Authorpreneur:
Making a Steady Income from Ebook Royalties

2015 International Edition

What are reviewers saying about the book?

"I have read literally dozens of books on self-publishing, book marketing, indies, etc. This is one of the best... hands down! And I read these types of books with the critical eye of a direct marketing consultant with over 40 years of experience."

"I've read several books about selling ebooks and this is definitely one of the best ones! Ms. James really speaks directly to the author in a down to earth way without using a bunch of big words or filler words."

"This book takes you from the writing stage to the publishing and marketing stage. It is a very comprehensive guide. It's perfect for someone just starting out as a self-published author or someone looking to breathe new life into their works."

Kristen James

Authorpreneur:
Making a Steady Income from Ebook Royalties

ISBN 978-1489591821

~ AUTHORPRENEUR PRESS ~

Kristen James has over 20 published works. Her books have hit the top 100 Bestsellers in Kindle US and Canada, #1 in eight different categories, and #1 in Movers & Shakers and free rankings. She writes women's fiction, romance and romantic suspense.

kristen@writerkristenjames.com

www.writerkristenjames.com

www.facebook.com/WriterKristenJames

https://twitter.com/writerkristenj

Amazon Author Profile and Full Book List:
http://amazon.com/author/kristenjames

Cover Design
Ramona Lockwood
http://coversbyramona.blogspot.com/

Contents

Introduction to the new 2015 International Edition

I'm very excited to share "Authorpreneur" with authors around the world in different languages. The term is a combination of author and entrepreneur to reflect that authors are business people, running a small company and handling writing, publishing and marketing. This book is about the business of being an author. It's wonderful to see the ebook markets in other countries developing and growing, giving opportunities to local authors and even international authors through translation. These days, you have even more resources available to aid you compared to US authors two and three years ago.

Publishing ebooks has changed the lives of many authors already. They're reaching new readers and making steady income from their writing. It's not just ebooks. More and more readers are buying print books online. You can also stock your print books in stores with some effort, and increase revenue streams through audiobooks and translations.

A Little About Me

I write "romance with a twist." I currently have twelve novels, ten novellas, and four nonfiction books such as this one. My books have ranked in the top 100 Kindle in the U.S., U.K., and Canada. Most of my books have a print version, and many of my novels have an audiobook and/or foreign language translation. I've self published the majority of my books, but I've also worked with publishers.

When I write a novel, I'm in the creative mindset. Afterwards, however, I publish the book and switch to a business mindset and see the book as a product. I think about promoting and maximizing income with different formats for each product. This book shares what I've learned about "packaging" a book product, marketing, and managing a writing and publishing career.

"Authorpreneur"

What is an Authorpreneur? This is the term that came into being within the last few years that encapsulates being an author and entrepreneur, and it covers terms such as self published author, Indie author and hybrid author. You could correctly say that traditionally published authors are entrepreneurs too.

In years past, every other industry esteemed people who started their own business, but not so in publishing... until now. Self publishing is becoming mainstream, Indie authors are earning a steady income, and self published books are hitting the #1 spots on ebook seller lists. In the last week of April 2013, five of the top ten ebooks were self published. The week before that, the #1 and #2 ebooks were self published. Some highly successful Indie authors are signing print-only deals with major publishing houses while others are choosing to remain self published and retain all of their rights. There are also hybrid authors that use the best of both publishing routes to achieve their goals and reach more readers. We have options now. The gatekeepers are readers. It's an amazing time to be an author and I feel so blessed to be a part of what is happening.

Like traditional publishing, self publishing has its mega bestsellers, big sellers, midlist authors and many authors hoping to join those ranks. Unlike traditional publishing, self publishing provides the opportunity for midlist authors to earn significant income from their work, even in niche markets or with a few thousand book sales per month because Indie authors get to keep a higher percentage of the profit. Indie bestseller Hugh Howey wrote that he's not the big story of self publishing—rather, it's all the authors making a living.

Today, many authors are earning a steady and significant income from ebook royalties. Who knows what you can do—the sky's the limit. But this isn't a lottery where you simply throw any book out in the wind. It does take work.

In this book, I aim to give you an honest, sometimes blunt, assessment of what it takes to grow your ebook royalties into steady income. That "income" may compliment your main income or contribute to your family's finances, or it might be the best money you've ever made. Being an authorpreneur is like running a small business, though: it takes time, dedication, and work. It also offers freedom and great emotional and financial rewards.

Part 1: Where Are You in Your Career?

I hope this book will be helpful to both beginning authors and authors with a few books under their belt. With that objective in mind, this first section will look at different issues and tips that will help you at different stages of your writing career.

Writing Your First Book
(Or first few books)

Let's say you're writing your first book or the first you think you will publish. (I wrote quite a few before my first published novel.) Maybe you even have one or two books out already—this section can help you too. I'll discuss ideas, writing, schedule, getting feedback and publishing.

The first advice I'm giving might go against the norm, but here goes. Remember all of this is about STORY first: characters driving plot. What draws in readers and sells more books than anything else? A grabbing idea. It's about that pure, consuming idea that won't let you go until you write the book.

What would happen if a teenage boy and an older woman were stuck on an island together for several years? *On the Island* by Tracey Garvis Graves.

What would happen if the witness to a murder had a multiple personality disorder? Could they be a suspect as well? *Multiple Wounds* by Alan Russell.

What if a husband made a promise to come back, and had to come back from death to keep that promise? *The Memory Thief* by Emily Colin.

All of these novels are much more complicated than the starting question, but that hook not only guides the author while writing, it hooks the reader.

Writing well is very important—don't get me wrong. But great writing won't sell an average story. Not to an editor or online browsers. On that note, let's talk about ideas.

Ideas

I get book ideas every day. Some I can toss out after a few minutes, while others I write down to simmer awhile. Some ideas work well in my head, but when I try writing out a summary, it's just not enough. It's possible to take an idea like that and blend or mix it with another idea. Sometimes it's best to just use it as a practice exercise and move on.

The big test, for me, is when I can *see* the idea. Near the end of 2012, I had an idea: what would happen if a couple was about to divorce and they found an orphaned baby on their doorstep? I could see this picture in my head, along with all the questions and implications. The storyline changed and developed once I began writing, but that initial flash of inspiration and excitement stayed with me.

Testing Ideas:

* Write what **you** want, what you dream about, what you want to read. Does your story idea keep you up at night because you're so excited? That will show!
* Don't follow the current 'hot' genre or book. By the time you can write a copy, the trend will be over or changed. Again, write what bubbles up from inside you.
* Is the story problem really big enough to carry a novel? I keep seeing little book promos on Facebook that don't actually sound like a story problem to me. For example: "Angie is fighting with her boss, her dad had a heart attack, her son is trying drugs, and worst of all: she's falling in love." To me, this isn't a bigger-than-life problem. It might work with a special slant, but the

description of falling in love as the worst problem doesn't grab me.

* Are you excited about the story idea or do you just think it will sell? If you're not hopping up and down excited, no one else will care either.
* Are there ways to further complicate the problem, add obstacles, and develop the storyline and characters?
* Does the story idea raise questions and make you wonder? This is the biggest selling point for readers. They see the description and it makes them wonder about all kinds of things.

Writing

To be a writer, you must write. The best way to get a book written to is have a goal and a road map.

I start with an idea, a flash that first inspires me to write the book, and I build from there. Normally I have a working book blurb at the beginning of my book file which guides me through the process. Sometimes, I even write the beginning *and* end of my books and then work my way through. So I'm a planner for the overall story, and how it opens and ends, and then I let things develop in the middle.

I don't think anyone can either write entirely according to plan or completely write on the fly. There has to be some planning, even if it's just a movie in your head. And you have to have some freedom and creativity as you write.

I think having a summary or outline will greatly assist you with your first few books. It can range from a one page summary of the story to a ten page, detailed outline, but it should be something to refer to when you wonder if you're on track.

There's an overwhelming wealth of books, blogs, and articles on how to write a novel. We also have millions of novels to study, too. I won't try to cover writing in depth since this is more of a trade book on the business of being an author. My advice is to make the story big, the stakes and changes big, and make it meaningful. Here I'll list a few quick tips that have really helped me as a writer:

Tips:
* Don't start with back story, a long description, a fake main character, a fake beginning that is supposed to pull readers in, or anything that isn't a part of the main story and conflict.
* Give characters both good and bad traits, but show your hero's good traits right away, so we can bond.
* To make characters interesting and quirky, ie memorable, look at their inner conflicts, pain and idiosyncrasies: beliefs at odds, loving opposites, wanting something desperately that will preclude other desires. That pulls a reader in much more than just an unusual hobby or habit, although those are good in fiction, too.
* Have your character drive the plot.
* Have an inner and outer conflict.
* Keep a journal to write about books that really amaze you and keep notes on writing. I used to take notes on paper and then would lose them. Now I write all my notes in a big, thick journal.

Schedule

If you want to finish a book within a few months, begin by tracking how many words you write a day. You can learn a lot about yourself by looking at how quickly you naturally write and your best writing times. I discovered I naturally write about 1500 words a day, although sometimes I get really excited and write up to 3,000. So I set a goal of writing 2,000 words a day, at least five days a week. If I skimp on one day, I can make up the words on another day, or that night after the kids go to bed. My goal keeps me focused so I can finish a 60,000 word novel in two months, while still enjoying the process.

You might like to write every single day or have a few hours every other morning or night. Stick to what works for you and track your progress. This is important because if you miss a few days or a full week, it throws you off your target date. It's also hard to get back into the story and groove of writing if you miss very long. Even writing 500 words a day, five days a week, will get you a 60,000 word book in six months.

Getting Feedback

There's many ways to get feedback on a manuscript, such as a critique partner or group, or posting works in progress on your blog or a social writing site. I know there's a worry out there sometimes that someone will steal your work, but honestly, I think we worry about that much more than we need to. Posting online is an option for those who feel comfortable with it.

Here's a fast but scary way to get honest feedback:

Give your completed manuscript to an acquaintance (not family or friends) with the instructions, "Pretend you paid ten dollars for this book. What would you say in a review?"

Preparing to Publish

Many writers know other writers who can help with editing and proofreading, especially if you're a part of a writing group. I've used the English site Guru.com to find editors and proofreaders. During 2014, I've seen project postings in foreign languages or duo languages.

Some writers hire several freelancers to critique their book, looking at plot and character development, dialogue, flow, and believability. This can also be called story editing.

Writers can request a story edit and then a line edit. The first edit looks at the big issues, moving or cutting scenes, cutting or changing characters, and rewriting chapters or sections. I'll be honest here: I did a lot of this in my earlier books, and now I just write the story and go through one edit. It used to take me a lot of wandering around before I really had a grip on the story. Now I see it in my head and develop it for a while before I write.

If you need to find a freelance editor, there's nothing wrong with having people apply for the job. You can post a project on Guru.com, Elance.com or a similar site in your country, and hire editors for a chapter. (Just don't post a project where you expect them to edit for free. It's not nice and the site actually prohibits it.) I hired several editors based on their reviews, experience, proposal, and the feeling I got from them. I wanted to work with someone I clicked with.

Here's what I looked for:
* Someone who will question things, such as timing, if something would actually work, if I gave a different impression of the character in a previous chapter, etc.
* An editor who notices details such as eye color, clothing, actions, etc. When you're self editing, it's easy to have someone start the day in a skirt and then end up in jeans, or to change their eye color, or have someone know something that they couldn't actually have known until later.
* An editor who challenges me. If anything is lacking in my story, I want to hear from my editor, not a reviewer on Amazon!
* And finally, someone who can make my sentences a little better and clearer when needed. I tend to put important information at the end of sentences and sometimes I switch words in a funny way, like hiking *books*, or 'put the car in the bag' instead of 'put the bag in the car.'

Tips:
* Hire a proof reader, or two or three. It's mind boggling how many tiny things pop up down the road, even after hiring people to check it.
* There will be tiny things that most people miss, except that one reviewer having a bad day.

* Learn from me and don't edit after proof reading. I have been horribly naughty about this. I'll have a book proofed and re-proofed, and when I get ready to upload, I'll look through it and make a tiny little change, and oops, there's a typo.

Publishing

The Publishing Section of this book will be very useful to you at this stage. It covers how to set up books for the maximum selling benefit.

What to Expect

I began self publishing with several novels, and I'm sure others' experience will vary, but I wanted to give you an idea of what can happen once you have a published ebook. (We'll talk about setting up books and promoting soon.)

First I need to say: the market will be different in different countries, and your genre makes a big difference too. There are many factors that will influence how well your book sells, including:

Title
Cover
Description
Genre
Your other books
Platform
Marketing
Reviews (on ebook retailers and book blogs)

Other factors beyond your control, such as a lucky mention on a big blog

You may find sales start slow at first and grow steadily, jumping up and down. When I started publishing several years ago, my sales were slow but growing for the first few months. After six months, sales started jumping:

50 ebook sales in June
100 in July
550 in August
1900 in September
3030 in October
3750 in November
10,000 in December

I didn't realize it at the time, but my timing was good. Ebook sales, at that time, dipped in the summer and grew as we headed toward Christmas. Since my first peak, my sales have tended to rise from June through December, with another big month in January. They slowed down through May and then started the process again. I started with a Christmas themed book, *A Cowboy for Christmas*, and I think that's benefitted my holiday bump. I added two more holiday novellas, so I might experience the summer dip more than other authors.

In 2013, I had a huge summer and a smaller holiday season bump, so sales can vary a great deal year to year and month to month.

If you'd like to see more real numbers, I found an interesting (English) blog called "Ebook Formatting Fairies." There was a post thereon April 12, 2013, that lists different authors who chose to respond and share their sales numbers for the last three years. It's available at:

http://e-bookformattingfairies.blogspot.com/2013/04/author-know-thy-business-self.html.

In their first year, most authors sold in the hundreds, and then moved up into several thousand copies sold the second year. However, one author reported selling 42,000 her first year. You'll see a range of 50 to 270,000 ebook sales in 2012 for different authors, with many reporting something like 50,000 copies sold.

This blog is especially useful because it shows how many books each author has, so you can also see that things really start to add up and snowball when you continue to write and publish.

Check out the quotes on this blog too–so many previously traditionally published authors are saying self publishing is a godsend. (The blog has many informative posts, and they offer ebook formatting services—worth checking out!)

Being an Indie author is a great way to add residual income to your total income and there is the definite possibility that the sales revenue will grow year to year.

I've had some books really sell and some that seem to tag along for the ride, so publishing is a bit of a gamble. You can put your best foot forward with a great story, writing, cover and marketing, and then it's time to evaluate how you're doing. This next section is about what to do if you feel sales aren't coming along the way you hoped.

What to Do When You're Feeling Stuck

You might get stuck after one book—you've been researching, marketing and tweaking, but you're not seeing the sales. Most authors need to publish several books before seeing real growth in sales. It's hard to do much with one book because:

* You're pushing the same thing over and over
* You only have one book out there to attract readers, and then there isn't a second one to buy
* Readers can be weary of a one-book author. It's not the biggest book buying factor, but it can sway some buyers
* You will learn and improve with more books, so it's natural for later books to sell better

The answer can be to move on to your next book. You can apply what you've learned so far and you have another chance to hit on a grabbing plot. Some books just sell better than others; every author sees this in their own work.

If it's been a while since you published your first book and you're in the early stages of working on your second, consider writing a novella. (See <u>Novellas</u>.)

Sometimes, there is a quick fix: the cover and book description. When authors email me about slow sales, I start by looking up their book page. Most often, I advise them to change their cover.

* A good cover has people on it. Does yours?
* Your cover should display colors and text fonts common in your genre so readers can instantly tell what your book is about.

Your cover needs to be eye-catching, but it doesn't have to show all the main elements in your story. Simpler is stronger and better. Take some time to look at the top sellers in your genre and the top 100. You'll notice color themes, certain fonts, and even themes with the people on the covers for different genres. It's possible that your cover has been telling the wrong information.

*Your description shouldn't summarize the book: it's sales copy. It should hit on the big points and raise more questions than answers.

What about your title? Yes, I've advised authors to change their title on certain occasions.
* Is it too long and confusing? Short and catchy is better. Your title doesn't have to explain the book. It does need to be memorable in order to sell.
Hopefully you can improve your book's sales page by adjusting your cover and description, but Indie authors have the option of changing the title if needed.

Another step to take is looking at your categories. I cover these more later, but keep in mind that you can change these. Maybe there's a similar category that still fits your book, and you can switch. It might be the category with your readers. It'll at least show your book to new people. There's been times when Amazon added subcategories, too. For a while, I couldn't get my Native American novel listed under Native American until some new categories were added.
Your keywords are another thing to look at. Maybe you can update them to match your book description better.

After looking at your book page, you can evaluate how you promote online. There are a few things authors do online that can annoy readers, and some of them are not too obvious. These refer to social marketing on Facebook, Twitter and other social sites:
* Is your profile picture your book cover? If you're wondering why this is bad, it separates you. You're no longer a person to interact with. It also signals that you'll be spamming and promoting the book, since it's obviously the purpose of your page.
* Are you posting a lot of reviews on Facebook or Twitter? The people following you already like your

work, so you're preaching to the choir. I know this sounds counterintuitive, but once I really limited my promotional posts, I watched my Facebook likes and book sales grow.

* Are you posting your sales numbers? It seems natural that your fans will be supportive of you, but sharing sales numbers can either look like you're bragging, or it might reveal you're selling much less than they thought. An occasional milestone post is much better than talking about your sales often.

* Are you posting when you get royalty checks? I don't think this is common but I've seen it, and I can't imagine that fans want to see posts on it.

* Do you post about politics, religion or other hot topics? Or display a negative attitude about anything? This includes talking about how difficult it is to get noticed as an author, selling books, getting reviewed, etc. (People want to follow successful people, so it just hurts your further to complain.) Your friends want to hear about that stuff, but fans want to hear about what you're writing, new releases, fun things about your life, and who you are as a person.

In short, remember your Facebook page or Twitter account is for interacting with fans (friends!) and sharing news. Another tip: it won't draw in readers or sell books to post links on other authors' pages. You'll just annoy that author, who will delete your post. You can be pretty sure their fans won't click on spam, either. There are much better ways to build a fan base online, which we'll discuss later in the book.

You can diagnose some problems by looking at reviews on Amazon and Goodreads. A low number of reviews means the package (cover, description, preview, and price) aren't enticing people to buy. This can be true for one or several books.

If you're getting bad reviews, you might be able to learn something from them. I don't mean just a few bad reviews. Everyone gets some bad reviews from people who don't even read the genre or even people who love to rip apart books because they're just not nice people. Take a look at the mean reviews on bestselling books. Everyone from Stephen King to Nicholas Sparks gets them. But they get many more positive ones than negative reviews.

Books that sell well tend to get a lot of good and bad reviews. But it can be a different story if you're not selling and the few reviews you get aren't favorable. Does a common theme emerge across Amazon and Goodreads? Do you see comments and know that yes, it's a problem?

I say all this with a grain of salt because, well, sometimes it seems like reviews don't mean anything. They don't always correlate to sales and we don't really know the source. I have a novel that is rated 5 stars in the UK and 3.4 stars in the US. It's also one of my higher rated books on Goodreads. The US reviews rip it apart like it's the worst book on the planet, yet it sells in the US and other countries. Readers who buy my other books tend to get that one too. So what can I take away from the US reviews? It's hard to say!

When sales aren't growing, it might be time to reevaluate what you're doing, in terms of the writing. It's possible you're trying to write to the market or what you think you *should* be writing. When I first I began, I wrote romances and tried to follow the rules set out by Harlequin and Silhouette. They had required word counts and rules to follow. I found myself struggling with the word count and getting the right level of sensuality. After I began self publishing, I decided to write what I wanted to read. I revised areas of my books where I had pushed myself to write more descriptive love scenes than I wanted. Now I always write exactly the tone I want, and I leave out details that I would skip when reading. While I love writing romance, I also realized that I want my books to extend beyond that and cover more of my character's life.

If you've published several books and aren't seeing sales—maybe less than 100 a month or they aren't growing from year to year—even after tweaking the packaging and other suggestions in this book, you have a few options:

* Switch genres. Is there something else you want to try? Maybe in a novella?
* Mix genres. Maybe instead of romance, you'll find you like writing romantic suspense.
* Invest more in your writing with a writing retreat or in-depth critique.
* Ask authors you trust to look over your book page on Amazon and book for suggestions.
* Take a look inside and really dig for emotions. Are you holding back in your writing? Editing out anything that might embarrass you? Reveal you? Embarrass others? What if you're editing out the truth of your story, or your writing voice, or that special spark that will connect with readers?
* Take a break from writing and promoting—go on a wild adventure and get inspired.

I'm throwing out a lot of ideas, I know. In the end, it'll be up to you to decide how long to pursue writing if the sales don't follow. Writing a book is an accomplishment, and it won't go away. I've had periods where it was hard to concentrate on writing. I didn't write a book one year because I wasn't focused. Sometimes I have to step back for my sanity and remember there's life outside of writing and publishing! You might walk away for a while and then one day get hit with a book idea so vivid, you have to run to the computer and begin writing.

Most writers will have a "stuck" period that passes or a time where they're frustrated and want sales to grow faster. We'll talk much more about marketing and growing book sales, so let's refocus on stages in a writing career.

Getting Sales Moving

Here's a few big ideas that can get sales moving:

* Put your entire backlist free for five days to promote a new release.

* Dump a few hundred dollars into Facebook ads to promote a new release, multi book freebie event, or giveaway

* Spend some time submitting to reviewers (more long term, and you need to network a bit beforehand)

* Publish a box set or an anthology with other authors

* Buy a promotion through an ebook site that promotes books. Just look at their results to see if the investment is worth it. Are their followers mainly other authors? That's a bad sign.

Making it through the Slow Times

I might repeat myself some in this book in my attempt to encourage and share information, but this is an important point: Every author has times when sales are slow. Things go up and down. The first time my sales slowed, after the holiday season, I thought the sky was falling. Then sales picked back up, and they've fluctuated, moving up and down like ocean waves. Something comes around, like a new release, holiday season or a paid promotion, and sales go back up. My "slow" months now were really good months back when I started, but sales haven't continually grown every single month. Every year, yes. That's why it's important to look at the big picture.

If things are quiet on the sales front, keep writing. More books means more promoting opportunities, but more than that, it's what you do. You're an author. You write books. Hopefully you're in this business because you love writing stories.

If income is a concern during slow times, you can earn money in other ways such as freelance writing, editing, speaking or something completely away from writing. I was freelancing before I wrote full time, and I still like to take on projects here and there. It's a different medium, and I enjoy writing nonfiction, so I can get pumped up that way.

You Have Several Books Published

It's an amazing and exciting time when you've written several books and are starting to really put everything together. Your writing voice is emerging in your work. You're developing a natural feel for story arch, character development, dialogue, and all the fun techniques we like to use. This was the time when I had some big 'Aha!' moments and saw something new about my writing, understood some things on a higher level, and began to develop my own tricks.

This is also when you begin to feel more like an author and know you can produce a book again and again. That's something readers look for, too, so you might even have a following.

Literary agent Donald Maass pointed out that authors reach a tipping point at five books. It seems to be when a writing career starts to build momentum. It shows readers that you're sticking around and building a career, and that you know how to write.

If you're not already, now is a good time to get involved in a supportive author group that matches your goals.

Tips:
* The <u>Publishing Section</u> will hold a few tips and tricks for you. Glance through and use it as a check list.
* At this point, a little fine tuning in your writing can make a big different in sales and gaining new readers. You might be on the brink of writing your breakout novel.
* You will see ups and downs in monthly sales due to the season, Amazon running a promotion, slack periods between new books, and times when you stepped back from marketing. Remember to look at the big picture, not just week to week sales.

* Decide what works best for you to track sales. It's critical to know if a promotion actually worked and to see trends from year to year.
* At this point with several books, if you have a great package (book, cover, blurb and formatting), you can really start selling.

Earning $500+ per Month and Growing

To someone outside the ebook publishing world, $500 a month probably doesn't sound like much. Income wise, it's not, but it's an accomplishment if you're earning that much each month from ebook royalties. It's cause for celebration, in fact, and a stepping stone to even bigger accomplishments. The big point here is once you get book sales going, they tend to grow.

My ebook sales have doubled from year to year, and my royalty income as tripled. There are two kinds of growth at play:

* The same books sell more copies and earn more money each year.
* We can add new books each year.

Through both of these, my reader base is growing.

Most books out there like this one will talk about marketing and how to grow your book sales. I'm offering a slightly different perspective on it. You see, the growth above isn't directly from marketing. The books themselves, and the new books I've added are finding new readers. A little visibility can go a long way in growing book sales.

These days, I'll release a new book or run a special on a big ebook site, and then I'll watch a ripple effect through my books. One will spike and then the increased sales filter through the other books. When a reader finds me and likes my writing style, they tend to go through all my books.

I know the competition is fierce out there. Then again, a reader doesn't stop at one book. You can get your books out there and grow name recognition. I've tried all kinds of marketing and methods, and I'll share my experiences with you.

Tips:
* Think long term for bigger results!
* It's been beneficial to my mental health to look at monthly and yearly trends instead of focusing on web hits and sales each day.
* Expect growth, but think of growth in business terms: most businesses grow month to month, year to year. A mom and pop store doesn't open and turn into Amazon overnight. We do have some huge Indie Author success stories, but many more writers are growing a readership and earning a very nice income. You can dream but make sure you set realistic expectations.

Look at trends in your writing to strengthen your author brand:
* If you write several genres, does one sell better than another?
* Do books with a certain theme sell better or get better reviews? I also listen to feedback from Facebook and emails. Many of my readers loved my romances with married couples who overcame problems. That might not work as well for other writers—sometimes it's the writing style and theme—but you can see by your reviews and sales if you hit upon something that works.
* Do you have any books with potential for a sequel or series? Sales pick up on a first book when you publish a sequel and then you have two that are selling.

Readers enjoy series and even books set in the same location such as a fictional town.

* Do you have a special slant to your writing? I set my books in Oregon because I love it here and I notice reviews talking about the beautiful setting. It's just a little way of setting myself a part. Maybe you have knowledge of a specialized job, a way of life, an exotic setting, or some other feature that can become a signature of sorts.

* Look at your social media to see what gets the best response. I know what gets readers talking on my Facebook page so it's become easier and easier to keep people engaged. You can go into your "Insights" on Facebook to see which posts get the biggest fan interaction. You can also see what promotions worked and what caused people to unlike your page.

* Do your book covers show your genre? Your subgenre? This is important in mystery and romance. (And probably other genres too.) There's a big difference between a light mystery and a gritty, violent one. In romance, there seems to be hundred of genres! Many romance readers like a certain level of sensuality, which is usually revealed by the cover. The spicier the cover, the spicier the writing. It's one way of telling the reader what to expect so they're not disappointed with their purchase. (It will still happen that someone will get your book expecting something it's not, but you can cut down on it.)

* Do you have a visual author brand? This is most apparent on your book covers. Take a look at Barbara Freethy's books and you'll see what I mean. This creates a theme on your website, and I have my covers across the top of my author page and on my Twitter page. On Amazon, the "Customers Also Bought" section on one of my book pages is often filled with my other books, so the theme even shows up there.

Taking Care of Business:

(This tax section is written for the US but the idea applies to other locations.)

Once you're earning money through self employment in the US, you'll need to make estimated quarterly tax payments. It's smart to talk to your accountant about tax issues, including what you can deduct. I keep an Excel sheet, with a new page for each month, of income and expenses, listing all business expenses, miles and earnings. Some people prefer Quicken or QuickBooks since this software helps you organize your expenses into marketing, business fees, etc. Find a system you like and track your income and expenses through the year. This way, so you're ready for tax time as a self publishing author.

Tax Tips:

* Record everything throughout the month. It's difficult to go back over a month or several months to find amounts and/or receipts.

* Miles add up! Count miles if you visit a client, drive to a book signing, drive to a conference or literary event.

* Supplies add up! You can deduct your printer, paper and other office supplies directly used for your writing.

* Ask your accountant about deducting for your home office, a percentage of your internet and phone.

Earning Thousands per Month

Once you're earning $1000, $3000, $5000 per month from your writing, it can change your horizons. You can see real possibilities here. You're getting to the level where your books are making money to put back into your future books instead of pulling from other income or savings. Some people can start living on their book royalties, especially if they have other income coming in. (Again, that all depends on if you're supporting others, if you have other family members contributing, and many other factors.)

At this point, you might expect things to tip. They could, especially if you keep writing. But, because the US ebook marketing isn't growing like it was, you might find yourself bobbing up and down here, making $3000, then $6000, then $2000, and maybe even having some low months where you earn under $2000. It can be unpredictable, and there's the possibility for a huge month at any time.

An older book might take off, and it's also true that a new book might go huge and then all of your older books will sell well. To continue growing, however, I advise adding several books a year. Don't spend so much time promoting existing books that you don't write new ones.

These days, I focus much more on writing than promoting. I'll publish a book and go back to writing the next one. Otherwise, I'm hyper-focused on promoting and watching my sales numbers, and it can drive me batty.

Writing the next book helps in other ways. Readers always want to know about the next book. So, even when you have a new release, it keeps people interested if you can mention something about your future books.

You also have freshly learned lessons to apply from writing the previous book too. I always learn something new when writing, and I have a certain excitement for creating story, a high that comes from finishing a book. On the flip side, sometimes I get a low in between books, wondering if I put all my heart and soul into the last one, so that I don't have anything for the new book. Then an idea comes along, and I find something new about myself that I can instill into the story.

There's just so many reasons to keep writing. If you set aside three months to promote a book, and don't start a new one, you have to get back into the writing mindset. Every author has their own method to writing and promoting, but I like to keep writing and spend a small amount of time on promotion.

When to Quit your Day Job

Many authors dream of making it big and quitting their job to write full time. I've always had that dream too. Instead of entering a different career, I studied writing and worked as a freelance editor, formatter, publisher and ghostwriter. I would have never ventured into writing nonfiction on my own if it weren't for all the articles and ebooks that I ghostwrote. I learned a lot about being brief, to the point, and convincing. It also taught me about business.

So I've always found a way to make it work to be self employed. I wanted to be here for my kids, and be flexible so I can be involved in their school activities. Still, I can imagine that it'd be scary to leave a regular job—and regular paycheck—for the unknown. (Steady income from royalties probably won't be consistent in the monthly amount.) I wouldn't even recommend doing so unless you've made enough with ebook royalties that you have six months, or least three months, worth of income saved.

You see, even if you have several big months, sales can drop again. Many businesses have a season, and publishing does too. There are months when you earn far more and can put away a large amount, and then months where you'll need to dip into that reserve. If you're considering leaving your regular job to be a fulltime writer, think about the low months in royalty earnings, not the highs. It might even be dangerous to consider the average if you're not one to save when you have high months. It's not all about money, either.

A word to the wise: the ebook market can change at any given time. 2014 was a year of huge changes in the US market, and many of these changes made it harder for Indie authors to sell books and earn as much. It can swing the other way just as fast. So it's important to understand that book income comes in lump sums and varies from month to month.

A few things to consider:
* Do you really want to be self employed?

* Do you have the discipline to keep to a writing schedule, promote online without spending all your time there, and find ways to connect with people locally outside of work?
* Do you mind working alone instead of with co-workers and people around? (It can get lonely at times.)
* Working part time can give you a social outlet and more time to write, while providing some consistent income.
* Can you buy health insurance? (If your spouse doesn't have insurance that can cover you.)
* Can you find work again if needed?
* Do you have other ways to earn money when royalties are low? (I freelance when I want to make money on top of royalties.)
* Can you adjust your life and spending if needed?

Of course your life situation greatly impacts how you feel about all of these items. There's a big difference between being the bread winner for a family of five verses being single. Maybe your spouse works, and you can add the icing to the cake. Many authors started that way, and later they're supporting the family. I've read quite a few stories of someone who was barely making ends meet, writing at night or early in the morning before work, and then they made it huge with ebooks.

Ironically, I chose the writing life because I had a family. I also have never liked having a normal job, with normal hours, getting up early, following orders... I'm more about saying 'yes' to opportunities than building a safety net. It's not that I'm addicted to taking risks, but I've stubbornly marched toward my dreams.

Some of you are coming to this from the financial and planning side, while others are driven by their dream of being an author. It's different strokes for different people, and I don't think there is anything wrong with that. I do want to give an honest appraisal of the work, time and money involved in self publishing, and guide those who want to write full time.

Let's Talk about "Success" and Numbers

From a business standpoint, if a book makes more money than you put into production and promoting, it's a success. You also need to pay yourself for your time. If you sell 5,000 copies of a book in a year, priced at $2.99 with 70% royalty, that can be a nice bonus. I think 5,000 copies is a beginning benchmark to show a book has commercial value. (Notice I define that as commercial – a book can be very well written and valuable without selling in the thousands of copies.)

5,000 is a good solid number in the US. In other countries with smaller ebook markets, it might be a bestseller at the number of copies.

10,000 copies is fantastic, especially within a year of release. If you're making a few dollars per book, that's a good year. (You can make anywhere from .35 cents to four or five dollars per book at prices that tend to sell.)

20,000 copies in the US, or worldwide in this day and age, is a breakout in my opinion.

My ebooks that sold 10,000 copies their first year continued to sell. There might be a different number in other markets, but reaching a certain saturation point seems to keep the book "alive" in ebook markets.

Important note: you can set goals based on actions such as "finish a book," or "write a blog post every week," but you can't actually set a goal of how many books you will sell. Certainly, you can look at return on investment in number of sales to determine if a promotion worked, but it doesn't work well to set your business goals on things out of your control. I set my goals with writing word counts, interacting on my Facebook page, blogging, and completing a promotion task each day which might include writing a newsletter, running a special, or something else I have control over.

Some authors bristle at defining success with income or just book sales. Indeed, there are many ways to define being successful as an author:

* Writing and publishing a book
* Winning a book awards
* Getting good reviews
* Getting a traditional book deal (even without making a lot of money)
* Making extra money
* Having a readership
* Earning residual income
* Making the New York Times or USA Today bestseller lists
* Being a household name
* Getting comments and emails from readers (I love this one!)

To be honest, I don't think any author would use just one of these criteria to define whether or not they're successful, and this list isn't comprehensive either.

I see success in levels and steps, and we should celebrate our milestones along the way. What's the point if we don't enjoy the journey?

Running the Numbers

We've established that each of us can define what we need to feel successful, so now let's talk about numbers and income. (This book is about working towards a steady income as an author, after all.)

Authorpreneurs look at publishing as a business, one that has expenses just like any other business. If you want to make real money from books, you need:

1. To invest in your writing career to improve your writing, which can mean a time investment and a financial investment.
2. To hire a good editor, proofreader and cover designer. These are not as expensive as some might think. There are many freelance professionals working through their own website and freelancing sites.
3. To learn about social marketing, although it's not that hard if you already use Facebook.

I invest $500 to $1000 on each of my books through the publishing process, and then an average of $100 per month on paid marketing. There are authors that spend much more than that for publishing and marketing, and some that find ways to save money so they can produce a professional book for far less.

Income

If one of your writing goals is to make an income from book sales, you'll first need to decide how much is "an income" to you. Do you need to replace what you make from your current job? Or can you adjust your lifestyle if you make less from your books? Do you have a budget that shows what you need to make every month to cover your expenses, and then spending and savings?

Some authors might not be trying for a full income either—maybe you have a number you need to earn to contribute to the family budget.

My budget shows me what I need to earn to "make it," and to be comfortable. The nice thing about ebook royalties is that I can see out for two months, so I have a two month warning if I need to earn some extra income through freelancing.

If you're starting out with a few books, you're probably not at a point where you can quit your job and write full time. (Of course there are all kinds of situations. Stay at home moms and dads that write, parents writing while kids are in school, people with alternate income or savings.) But let's assume most authors won't be able to rely on income from just a few books, even traditional authors.

To get an idea of possible income, let's look at selling 500 copies a month. I think it's a good beginning number to shoot for, and very reachable with just a few books.

I'm going to take you through several scenarios with 500 ebook sales a month and then I'll put them together in a graph so you have a visual, which will also show how much you can make if you sell more than 500 copies.

Averaging 70 cents a book at 500 copies

If you price a book at 99 cents on Kindle you'll make 35 cents per book, but you can also qualify for borrows under Kindle Select. Using this model, I generally earn 70 cents per book sale on average for my 99 cent books. The 35 cents profit is a set number, but the 70 cents is going to vary. You can also end up with an average of 70 cents, or higher, if you have multiple books and some are priced higher.

Taking the higher number, 70 cents, you'd make $350 a month by selling 500 copies.

*If you're having trouble selling ebooks at higher prices, consider writing 99 cent novellas with word counts of 10,000 to 40,000. If you write novellas in a series, you can sometimes even use the same cover image with different text. More on novellas soon.

Averaging $1 at 500 copies

In this case, you might have 3 to 7 books, priced from 99 cents to $2.99 or even higher. With an average of one dollar per book, you'd make $500.

I know: you might not sell the same number at each price point; this isn't an exact science. I have noticed that I seem to average around the same per book from month to month, until I add a book and change things, and then my average goes up. My average has been going up since I started because, as I add more books, I price the newer ones higher. That's another way to grow your royalty income.

Averaging $2 at 500 copies

If you price your ebooks at $2.99, you'll make a little over $2 per book, and you'd make $1000. You can get a $2 average with some 99 cents books, 2.99, and a few at 3.99. The cut off for novels seems to be about $4.99, in my opinion. Amazon allows you to price up to $9.99, so $4.99 is about in the middle. Look at other books in your genre and consider your book's length—longer books should naturally be priced higher.

In today's market, it can feel scary to publish a book at a higher price. When sales slow down, it's tempting to lower the price. That's why it's nice to have a backlist. I currently have a perma-free short read, quite a few 99 cents novellas and novels at $2.99. I started with lower prices with the long term plan to continuously add new books at a slighter higher price. I feel comfortable doing that because I'm growing as a writer and improving, and new readers can try my books for free or 99 cents.

When my sales spike or dip without a promotion, it's across the board and price points. You can get sales going by dropping the price to 99 cents, but sometimes it's just a slow week or month. Book sales slow in the summer and climb in the fall for both 99 cents books and $2.99.

		Number of book sales				
		500	1000	1500	2000	2500
Average	.70 cts	$350	700	1050	1400	1750
$	$1	$500	1000	1500	2000	2500
Per book	$2	$1000	2000	3000	4000	5000

Okay, here's the graph I promised showing the average price down the left hand side and the number of book sales across the top. If you sell 2500 books a month at an average of $2 per book, you'll make $5000. To achieve this, you probably have five or ten books with a mix of price points, and they're mostly selling well. Or you might have a few books and one really took off.

The beauty of this is, once you reach a certain level, things really start to snowball. You might have the normal slow season, but each holiday season will be bigger and bigger. Your low months will begin to look pretty good, too.

The average salary (according to a few articles I found on Google) in the US is $30,000, or $2500 a month. You can make that on ebooks if you sell 1250 ebooks a month at $2.99, following the Kindle pricing model. For some, this is enough to leave their day job and write full time, depending greatly on where you live and your income needs. In a two income household, it sounds even better. Or this might be your side job—and 20 or 30 grand a year for writing in your free time is pretty nice.

There are many different pricing strategies, which I'll go into later in the book. This is simplifying things, of course, and royalties tend to go up and down. The ebook season starts to pick up a little in July and August, starts really gaining steam in September and October, and then November, December and January are big.

Pricing Tips:
* Another way to get more per book sale is a box set. I have my first four romances together in a box set for

4.99. Interestingly, both the separate books and the box set sell.

* Pricing is the beginning of a strategy. Many authors change their price—dropping it for a few weeks and then raising it—to get sales going. I think it's the price change, along with the additional promotion you can then do, that gets sales moving.

Planning Book Sales Numbers

This is a trick heading—you can't plan how many books you will sell. You can plan how many you'll write, how often you'll blog, how much money you will budget for marketing, and so on. There's all kinds of things you can plan, but your sales aren't one of them.

This is where common sense and good financial advice come into play. Most people want to have a cushion or emergency fund set aside. When you have big months, I think it's always a good idea to save some. (It's a good idea to save every month.)

Sometimes it seems that here in America, our culture teaches us that once money starts coming, it keeps coming. We can spend it as soon as it comes in, and then borrow even more. The thing with writing is, you might hit a certain level for a while, but it could change. If you're self employed, you have to be ready for anything.

I hope that's not too sobering—I love being self employed. I just want others to understand the full picture and not just the glamorized version.

Part 2: Publishing

Print and Ebooks

These days, many authors wonder if they should bother with a print version of their book. Economically, having a print version might not pan out, but I set up print versions for other reasons. I love having a copy of my book in my hands, and having copies to give out to friends and family. Some authors still like to have book signings. There are a few readers who prefer reading in print, who will order your book from Amazon. So it just makes sense to have a print version, especially since you can publish through Createspace for free.

I guess I'm a bit backwards on the order. I'll set up my ebook first, publish it, and then work on the print. The ebook is the one that sells online, so I keep my focus there.

I've formatted over 500 print books so I can set up a print version within a day, once I have the ebook done. You just need to add the spine and back to create a wrap around cover for print. Most cover designers will make a wrap around cover for a little more, after they've created an ebook cover.

Exclusive with Kindle Select?

Amazon's Kindle Select program has been available to American authors for several years. It's a program where you commit to only publish ebooks through Amazon Kindle, and in return you get several benefits.

To enroll, you simply click the enroll button in your Kindle dashboard. Later, you can click on "manage benefits" to schedule a free day or Kindle Countdown deal. You can also click on "Details" and then select whether you want to auto-renew your enrollment every three months. If you plan to try out the program, be sure you uncheck the auto-renew box.

When the program first came out, I immediately joined. I'm glad I did because it helped me reach Kindle readers and gain visibility. However, now I have only a few of my books in Select. I've changed my goals and plans, so now most of my novels are in expanded distribution, meaning I can publish them on every site that I choose.

I wanted the freedom to publish on sites outside of Amazon because I'm using Babelcube for translations. I also wanted to reach readers who read on a Nook or other ereading devices. And for me, borrows had fallen off and weren't increasing sales. (Other authors have had different experiences.)

Being in Select is a personal decision for each author. If you're new to ebook publishing, and want to publish on just one platform, it might be a good option for you.

Enrolling in Kindle Select gives you the ability to have up to 5 free days per 90 day period. Amazon Prime Owners can borrow your book, and you get a percentage of the borrow fund, usually around $2. (It's been less in 2014 as the program expanded.) Now there is Kindle Unlimited which gives readers even more options for getting ebooks.

When I originally published this book, borrows had made up 26% of my royalty earnings. Borrows took my per book average profit up too, because the retail price of many of my shorter works was 99 cents. I used to advocate for using Select for the borrows and free days, but then the benefits began losing value. Putting a book for free would spike paid sales afterwards, but that hasn't happened for over a year now.

If you visit Authorearnings.com (English), you can read through a survey about how being in Select affects author earnings. The latest conclusion from October 2014 is that it actually hurts earnings for most authors in the U.S. Kindle market. The very top, and most visible authors, make a lot while most others are losing readers and sales on other platforms.

See the report at:

http://authorearnings.com/report/october-2014-author-earnings-report-2/

However, this information is based on the American market, and Select may be a good option in other countries. I think it depends on how many ebook platforms are available to you for publishing. If you only plan to use Kindle, Select is a great way to gain visibility and earn more royalties from borrows.

Assisted Self Publishing?

Before moving on, we should talk about all the assisted self publishing companies and services out there. Even large, traditional publishing houses are opening a self publishing section. These companies don't do anything beyond what you can do on your own. They sell marketing packages, but there are thousands of stories out there from authors who spent thousands of dollars with nothing to show for it. "Let's Get Digital" published a post about the business of making money on authors at:
http://davidgaughran.wordpress.com/2013/05/04/the-author-exploitation-business/.

Authors have been tricked into thinking that if they spent enough money with these companies, their books would be marketed and they'd "make it." There are legit self publishing services such as editors, proof readers, cover designers, and even companies that help you self publish, if they don't charge an arm and a leg.

How do you tell the difference? I offer freelance publishing services for authors where I format their book and help them publish a print and ebook version. I set them up so they can manage their own Createspace account. I charge a few hundred dollars, not a few thousand. That's the big tip off.

My point? There's just no reason to pay thousands of dollars to get published. You only need to pay for services when you need help.

You can check self publishing services in *Choosing A Self Publishing Service 2013: The Alliance of Independent Authors Guide,* available at
http://amzn.com/B00CC0NYCM.

I also follow Writer Beware on Facebook
(https://www.facebook.com/WriterBeware) for interesting articles and industry updates, along with things to watch out for.

Help Your Book Sell Itself

What do I really mean by this? Imagine going into a bookstore and looking around. There are some books that catch your eye. You pick them up, read the back, then flip through the pages. These books do not have the author sitting there, selling you the book (unless they're having a book signing) but the book sells itself much of the time. Your ebook needs to do the same thing, but in a different selling environment and with more obstacles to overcome. There are no guarantees that a reader will browse by your ebook and happen to see the cover. However, there are ways you *can* get your cover in front of potential readers. That's what this section focuses on. Many of these steps are very quick and easy, but I included every step because I see many authors overlooking them.

The next section is on strategies to sell more books, but I want to share one tip here. Outside of the actual writing, your package (book page, cover, description and preview) are what sells the product. If you publish a great story, that's well written, and has attractive packaging, it will pick up sales momentum. Let's start with your cover.

The "tiny" Cover

A book cover is that first look – you know when you see someone in a crowded café that makes you do a double take? It's like that. Every time you see a new cover, within that first second, you either become curious or dismiss it outright. So how do you develop that magical cover that will intrigue readers?

The color and feel of the cover is a big factor in buyer perception. This varies by country, but in the US, you might notice:

* Yellow covers signify a book on happiness, self help, improvement, or possibly a story of overcoming.
* Red and black, with stark contrast or bold lines, tells us it's a thriller or a hardboiled mystery
* Gray, mist, werewolves, castles... paranormal covers have a certain feel and there are sub genres in this category, too. Look around at covers that match your story type to see what readers expect.
* A couple shows romance and all the sub genres have cover themes. Readers look for these themes, so it's good to know what matches your story, no matter what you write.
* You can build on a genre theme by customizing it to your author brand. More on this later.

Good cover designers are experts at using genre, color, and tone to create a catching cover. Just google "cover designer" and you'll see you are spoiled for choice.

Take some time to browse through different sites to find a designer's style that really clicks with you. Many sell premade covers that are genre specific and surprisingly can match many different books. You can buy a premade cover and have the text changed, and you can usually have a few small elements changed as well, for free or a small fee.

I've bought premade covers and some that were customized from a stock photo I liked. The one thing to look for, which I always haven't, is whether the cover will be reused or not. It's a little disturbing to happen across a book by someone else that looks just like one of your own. I've seen the same images from a couple of my covers on other book covers, too. That's why I checked into it and decided to go with something more customized.

When you're designing your cover (working with a designer) ensure your cover looks great when it's half an inch by half an inch. Your cover needs to grab the reader's attention when they spot it in search results or in that section called "Customers also bought." Shrink the cover down to see how readers will see it at first.

Yes, some readers will see it on your site or Facebook where it may or may not be larger, but most of your new readers will spot your cover on Amazon. Go browse the bestseller lists and look at tiny covers. Check out the suggested books on every book page.

Often, my "Customers Also Bought" section is filled with my other books, so it helps to have multiple books out with a theme to the covers. It's really nice if you can run a book promotion on a book and have your books across that line too. That way you're not advertising for other books. There's another section down toward the bottom of the page where you can see what people bought after viewing that book. It's what they decided to buy *instead* of the book on the page. I've noticed people will look at one of my books and then buy another, maybe because it shows up in the "Also Bought" section.

Tips:
* Your cover will have a huge impact on your sales – hire someone to design a professional cover!
*Make your cover attention grabbing in small form
* Design your cover to reveal the story's tone.
* A simple cover will show up better in search results, "Customers also bought," and category listings with pictures.

Should you spend money on your cover?

(Cover, editing and proofreading)

This is a bit redundant, but it's so important. You might be thinking you just don't have $50 to $100 to spend on a cover. I wanted to share something with you. I can make two lists of my books: how much I spent on the cover, and how well they've sold. The titles would be in the same order on both lists. It's clear that what you spend on the cover (and editing and proofing for that matter) directly relate to what you'll make on the book. I know I owe much of the success of my holiday novellas to the covers.

I spent the most on the cover for *A Cowboy for Christmas.* It was before there were designer websites all over the internet, and I used Google images to find a picture of a woman with long, dark hair and a tall cowboy. It took a little looking, but I saw the painting and *knew.* Luckily the picture was on a painter's website, so I emailed her to ask about using it for a book cover. She hadn't licensed a book cover before, but we worked out a deal for a few hundred dollars.

I added the red (for Christmas and romance) and text myself, again because there weren't designers advertising everywhere. Now I wonder if the book would be doing even better had I hired a designer for the text. It adds that tiny bit of final polish that makes such a big difference.

More than Memories is right behind in second place for sales. It has a bit of a story. This one did start out with a cover I made myself, but then I replaced it with a new cover once I discovered there were so many talented designers that charged under $100. *More than Memories* is a little longer and has a higher rating, so I have to wonder if it could have outsold *A Cowboy for Christmas* early on if it had a better cover.

Here's the new cover for *More than Memories.*

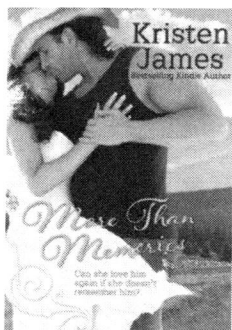

I've seen authors that didn't invest in the cover or production of their novels. Some of them spike their sales in December only to get a rash of bad reviews in the following months, knocking them for all the errors or bad formatting.

There are two production cycles for your book: the writing and story developing, and then the publishing. Even I had a lot to learn about how both cycles are equally important to building a lasting writing career. If you have a great story but skimp on any production steps, it can stop sales from taking off, make sales drop off, or even kill your career in its tracks. You can recover, but imagine if you get momentum going and then lose it because you rushed. Many of the Indie authors that have several books out now learned this as they went, but now self publishing is mainstream, and people look for quality books, no matter how they were published. All books are competing, and that means you have to look just as professional as Stephen King, Nicholas Sparks, Kristin Hannah, Nora Roberts, and the big names in your genre. The good news is that it's not that expensive to produce a quality book, and it's well worth it if you plan to stay in the game.

You can find countless cover designers these days with a portfolio of premade covers. Sometimes one is perfect for your book, and they often cost only $35. Even spending a little more for something custom is well worth it, and not that much at all!

I've always loved art and feel I had somewhat of a natural eye for designing book covers. I've hired several designers, but I've also made many too, both for myself and others. As you publish more and more, you'll probably develop an eye for what sells, and what matches your brand.

Cover options include:
Buying a premade cover
Hiring a designer to customize one of their ideas
Hiring a designer to start with your description/vision
Finding your own artwork or stock art and then hiring a designer to work with it

Make Your Title Short and Catchy

*Note: my examples are in English so the translated titles might not be as "catchy." Look over the top selling books in your own country and language to get a feel for what works.

After the cover art, the next thing most readers see is the title. If you go to Amazon.com and check the bestsellers, you'll find most titles are short. Great titles capture the book's essence.

For instance: *The Hunger Games*. That's pretty clear.

One of my favorite authors, Kristin Hannah, uses short titles like *Home Front, Winter Garden,* and *Between Sisters.* Her titles are usually two words that can sum up an entire women's fiction novel.

I like catchy titles, I admit it. You may have noticed this with a couple of my books – *A Cowboy For Christmas* and *More Than Memories.*

I love titles that are short saying, implying an understood meaning that can be developed within the story develops for a more specific meaning. Several books have used the title *Chances Are*. It's a fun, chick-lit title that you can slant in several directions.

One of the books on my keeper shelf is *A Bend in the Road* by Nicholas Sparks. It ties into a physical event in the story, and the entire novel is about a bend in the character's life. To me, that adds another layer to the story and it still offers a catchy title.

The top three ebooks for the week ending April 28th, 2013, were *The Hit, Damaged*, and *The Bet.* (The last two are self published.) You see, the title doesn't have to explain the entire book. It's a selling tool that should grab reader's attention and then allow you to build on the central idea throughout your novel.

Tips

* Make your title short, meaningful, and memorable.

* Use keywords in your title. You might have noticed I have "cowboy" in two titles and "Christmas" in three.
* If you do something different, know the rules and how to break them. Some genres have longer titles but it works.

Copyright Page as a Sales Page

With ebooks, you want to keep your front matter fairly short so readers can easily get to the preview. I like to list the copyright info, my website, Facebook, and list of other books with a link to my Amazon profile. I used Bitly at http://bitly.com/ to get the shortened link. You can also get a short link on your Author page on Amazon, as long as you've set up an account with Author Central.

After the basic information, you can list any awards and a few reviews. Highlight your strengths here – if you have a lot of books, list them. If you have just a few books, paste in your best reviews. If you wrote a nonfiction book and you're an expert on the subject, provide a short, professional bio.

Some authors like to insert the book blurb. This helps if people buy your book and read it later down the road. The blurb will remind them what the story is about.

I have links in my box set to the different books, and sometimes I'll have a link to the preview at the end.

You can be creative and find even more ideas to help sell your books; just remember to keep it to short so it doesn't take up your preview.

Formatting

You can get off to a good start by reading through Kindle's formatting guide. It's available on Kindle for free as a Kindle ebook at: http://amzn.com/B007URVZJ6.

You can get a PDF version for Windows or Mac right inside your Kindle account. Log in and go to the bottom of the page. Click "Terms and Conditions" and you will get to a page with links all along the right side under "Help Topics." If you click on "Building Your Book for Kindle," it'll give you links to download instructions. (The link underneath is the one to download a PDF.)

I'll also go through some of the most common mistakes here and ways to make your life much easier when formatting and converting books.

Bad formatting can be a deal breaker. Some bad formatting will show in your Word file, including spaces between paragraphs, disappearing tabs, font changes, or jumbling of texts together. These problems can occur in the converting process.

You might think it's not a big deal to have spaces between your paragraphs, but it annoys readers. I've seen quite a few discussions on Facebook about it, from dedicated readers. Some readers will ignore a few things they don't like, but you don't want to give them any reason to not buy or to stop reading. It's less common, but I've also seen a few books that went with the block paragraphs, where there is no indent and it has a space between paragraphs instead. This isn't a way around fixing the indents. The space between paragraphs works for a nonfiction book, but it's distracting in novels.

I write all my books in page size 5x8 with .5 inch margins. I set my paragraphs to .3 but you can do .5. Make sure to set your indent with automatic formatting – never the tab bar! And do not use spaces to indent paragraphs either. These two tips will save you hours of frustration when you convert.

After all the formatting, editing, and proofreading, when I know my book is ready to do, I save it as an html file. This will clear out the hidden formatting tags that create those annoying problems: the odd spacing, disappearing indents, etc.

First create a new folder to save in to and label it "Kindle files" or something that will make it easy to find. Then open your book in Word and save it as a "Web page, filtered" into the folder. You'll get an html file and a file with the pictures. Right click this file and "Send to" a zip file in the same location.

When you publish, choose this zip file when you upload your book. The html file will look strange on your computer screen, but it'll look really good in the Kindle preview during set up.

Formatting Tips:
* Keep it as clean and simple as possible for Kindle. Why? The text needs to flow, and people will change the font size. You don't want things looking crowded or messy.
* Insert a page break **right after the last line of every chapter.** (Hit Control and Enter to insert a page break.) Don't have a bunch of spaces and then the page break. This ensures you won't get a blank page in your Kindle file after conversion.
* Check formatting by clicking the little paragraph sign at the top of the page, in the paragraph tab. It will then show formatting marks, including tabs and page breaks.
* Don't use spaces or tabs to indent.
* Make paragraph changes in two places: under the paragraph tab up top, and under the "Normal" style. Otherwise a setting can sneak in and mess up the file.
* Be careful when editing. I once had an editor that preferred to use the highlight text feature or to change the font color instead of using Word's tracking features. I didn't know it was a problem until sometime later, when readers reported that there were missing words and paragraphs in some of my books. I had

changed the text back to "black" and not "automatic," so if someone read the ebook on a black screen, certain words disappeared.

A Winning Description

Your book description on Amazon is a sales page, not a book summary. That might surprise some people. Readers want to know THE BIG QUESTION, what's at stake, and why they should read the first page. They don't really care, up front, about the plot points in the middle of the book that will get them from point G to point T.

Think of your Amazon book page as:
* An elevator speech – the best of the book in 30 seconds
* A movie commercial
* A chance to show the book's writing style

A few tips:
* Don't write a huge chunk of text that will scare off readers –break it up.
* Don't try to explain the entire book.
* Don't explain sub plots or more than the main characters.
* Do give readers the big issues and character flaws.
* Cut fluff words such as adjectives to make the writing stronger.
* Add an excerpt from a review.
* Add a tiny sneak peak from an exciting or important scene in the book. It just has to make sense by itself and pull readers in.

A note on this last tip: adding a sneak peak is a good way to showcase your writing style and the tone of the book. I know readers can use the See Inside feature to read the beginning, but the sneak peak can show that you can write well throughout the book. If someone comes along, and for some odd reason, writes a bad review and rips apart your writing, a sneak peak can show that the writing is indeed worth reading.

Below is the blurb for my novel, *More Than Memories*, which shows the big conflicts and raises a lot of questions:

Can she love him if she can't remember him?

Molly Anderson returns "home" to a town she doesn't remember, hoping it will spark a memory. She runs into Trent Williams, an off duty police Detective, and something else definitely sparks.

He wants to know why she left town, with her parents, but without a word to anyone. She doesn't remember that life. She can only tell him she knew her parents briefly before they died . . . or were murdered, she's not sure. She hopes regaining her memory will help answer that question.

Trent has his own secrets, but they have a mystery to solve. As they work together and Molly meets their old friends, she realizes their relationship went deeper than memories. In fact, she grew up in Ridge City, even though her parents had said they lived there just a few years. How could she have forgotten her lifelong friend and love? Can she love him again if she doesn't remember him? There's also the possibility that she did something awful -- and maybe that's why she's afraid to remember her old life.

Molly knows she wants him now, but the truth might destroy their love.

***

I write romance, so I try to give a potential reader a glimpse at the conflict for both the heroine and hero. What is the big conflict for each of your main characters? What do they have to lose? What are they after?

The BIG hook, and what should define your sales page, is
* the big goal
* the must save
* the "can't lose"

* the big what if

Tip:
*Write a novel description that offers more questions than answers.

Nonfiction Tip:
Write a description that shows how your book solves a problem or will make life better.

If you're having trouble with your description (blurb), ask yourself if you're telling too much. I've gotten muddled down trying to decide which details to reveal. When you're close to the book, it's easy to try and explain the main plot, the character's relationships, and who the characters are. The reader wants a quick label for the characters and a few plot questions. They understand that you'll develop the initial blurb into a much bigger story, but at this point you just want to intrigue them.

Winning Categories

When you set up your title with Kindle Direct Publishing, you get to choose two categories. Some people will advise you to pick the two categories that you think you can rank in, even if it doesn't fit the book well, but this is likely to backfire. It makes it harder for the right readers to find your book, and the "right readers" are the most likely to actually buy your book when they come across it.

Instead, try to find the two categories that your book best fits into. Amazon helps readers find books by suggesting books in the genre they read. If you try to trick Amazon and readers with mismatched categories, it'll bite you in the end.

During the set up, you can click on most categories to open them and display sub categories. The more you can specialize, the fewer books are in the sub categories. This makes it easier to rank, and you are targeting people looking for exactly what you're offering. It also puts you into more categories, which not too many people know. When my romance books rank, they sometimes rank in a category that I didn't choose during set up. I get as specific as I can when choosing categories, but my books will still rank in romance and contemporary romance. Why? Because the specific sub category I chose was under romance.

Ranking in Categories

I'd like to include a side note here on promoting. Many authors will post when they rank in a category. It's exciting to authors…but you can go overboard.

For example, an author posted on Facebook that they were ranked #25 on Amazon. I thought, wow, I should check it out. It turned out their book was ranked #25 in three subcategories down and something like 50,000 overall. Posting that might get readers to the book page but it doesn't seem likely that they'll buy the book when it's not ranked what they thought.

When you start selling, it's not too hard to rank in a category and your Facebook fans might get tired of seeing posts about it. They might unlike your page over too many "look at this!" posts. I try to save those kinds of posts for big accomplishments so I'm not pushing my books to fans that already liked my page. You can also use that kind of info in your bio that way new readers see it in your books or when they look at your Amazon page, if you use the same bio in both.

I've noticed most fans engage more with posts about what's in the book—ie, the story—and things like your writing process, a big milestone, funny pictures, fun events, things to share about your life, and new releases. Too many posts about how well you're selling or ranking hurts your page. Just my two cents!

Winning Keywords

During setup, you can choose up to 7 keywords. Use all 7 for maximum exposure.

You might have heard of the two different kinds of marketing: shotgun and rifle. A shotgun sprays a bunch of tiny bullets. A rifle shoots a single, targeted bullet. In this day and age of endless information on the internet, you want to use the rifle method. The more specific you can be with anything online, the more quality traffic you will get. By hitting your exact target audience, you will get a higher purchase rate. You don't want to market to every reader. You want to market to readers who are likely to buy your book.

The 7 keywords for my romantic suspense novel *More Than Memories* are:

amnesia romance
detective romance
police romance
high school sweethearts
childhood sweethearts
romantic suspense
sweet romance

These are specific and directly related to the story; they're much better than just "romance" or "suspense."

Some people might enjoy contemporary romance but not romantic suspense. There's also a big difference between a "hard boiled" mystery and a light mystery.

The key is to hit keywords that people actually use to search for their favorite kind of books.

Many people advise to put your main keywords in your book blurb too. If you chose relevant keywords, you might do this automatically. For instance, my cowboy books have the word cowboy in the blurbs.

For nonfiction, think of the problem and solution such as:
Low book sales..... increase book sales

Hair loss.... hair regrowth, hair growth
Bad credit score.... raise credit scores

One last tip: You can use these same keywords on your website or blog.

Sub Categories using Keywords

You can enter your book into even more categories with certain keywords. Visit https://kdp.amazon.com/help?topicId=A200PDGPEIQX41, scroll down and click on your main category for keywords that will trigger a sub category.

For instance, if you use contemporary romance as a category and "college" as a keyword, your book can rank in New Adult romance when it's high enough in the rankings. Other keywords include wedding, Christmas, second chance, pirate, and firefighter. Getting into these sub categories gets you even more exposure.

End Matter

End matter includes your author bio, full book list, and links. You can even include book covers, as long as you create a zip file when you upload to Kindle. (See Formatting.) This is your chance to connect with the reader on a personal level and give them ways to connect with you online and find more of your books.

I include my photo, bio, book list with a short link to my Amazon author profile, and a list of books with their cover, blurb, and a short link to their Amazon book page. (I'm skipping this step in this book, and not including promos for my novels, since my other books are romance. The point of this book is to help other authors. You might sometimes have a good reason not to include all the bells and whistles.) The short links are important because they look more professional and they cut down on clutter. I've gotten short links from https://bitly.com/ and right off of Amazon. You can get a short link to your author page off the page itself, in the right hand corner, and you can get short links to your books under the link that says, "Tell us about a lower price." (I have no idea why they put the short link there, but that's where I found it.)

Many readers will simply google the author's name if they loved a book, but you can also provide multiple ways and links for them to connect with one click or buy with just a few clicks. Why not take advantage of that?

The end of the book is also where you can experiment. It won't cut into your preview to add content. I sometimes include a sample chapter of another book, but I also mention this in the front. Readers can get touchy about thinking they're 95% through the story when they reach the end. It helps to keep any sample content short in the end.

Author Profile

You can set up your Amazon Author profile through Author Central at
www.authorcentral.amazon.com. This is where you set up your photo, bio and book list. If you're not using this useful site, you're missing out. It shows all your reviews and sales in one place.

Author Photo
Your author photo should be professional and high quality, but you can have a little fun with it too. Make it reflect you and your personality.

I tend to use the same photo, or just two photos, across my platforms on Amazon, Facebook, Twitter, LinkedIn, and Wordpress. I like to use fairly recent photos, meaning less than a year or two old. (I do think it's okay to switch in a different photo sometimes for a fun occasion.)

A few tips for your photo:
- Don't use an old one. Quite a few times, I've talked to someone on FB or Twitter, and later saw a different photo of them and realized they were 20 or 30 years older than I thought. I don't think I'm the only one who doesn't like that.
- Don't use your book cover. There is nothing more annoying than talking to a book cover on FB, Twitter, or another site. This is your author personality! It should be a person.

Tip: "Dress for the job." Make your author profile look and sound like it the successful author you want to be.

Author Bio
You don't have to use the same bio across the board. I use a short, yet personal bio in the backs of my books. If the reader is reading my bio, that means they probably enjoyed the book.

So I don't try to be overly impressive—I just want to share some interesting things about myself.

Here's one of the bios I've used in books:

Kristen James was born and raised in Western Oregon and sets most of her stories there, in an Oregon small town, the rugged mountains, or on the beautiful coastline. She enjoys the outdoors and watching wildlife in her yard and along the river by her house. Besides reading and writing, she loves traveling, cycling, hiking, berry picking, canoeing, fishing, and camping, especially doing all these with her family. Life should be an adventure!

Here's a short bio that I use on my website (in conjunction with a longer bio) and any guest blogs or articles I write:

Kristen James has over 20 published works. Her books have hit the top 100 Bestsellers in Kindle US and Canada, #1 in eight different categories, and #1 in Movers & Shakers and free rankings. She writes women's fiction, romance and romantic suspense.

Tips:
* Your bio can tell more about you as an author and a person. Share what makes you tick, why you write, and what has shaped you as an author and person. Be creative!
* Mention your other passions besides writing.
* What led you to write?
* Did you have another career before writing? Or lead a very different life?
* If you were to visit a talk show, how would you like to be introduced?
* What makes you fun, intriguing, mysterious, or different?

Pricing That Sells

This might be the most debated topic in Indie publishing. It's a constant game in publishing and any other industry for that matter. How do you find the perfect point where your product will sell and yet you still make a profit?

When I began with a few romances, I played around with price and found I could sell the most books at 99 cents. It seemed at times I could make the most money at that price because I sold many more copies. And profit wasn't the big issue then. I wanted to reach as many readers as possible and grow a fan base. Borrows came along and raised my earnings for each title. I added a box set for the same reason, plus it gave me another Kindle Select title with five more free days.

These days, in 2014, I'm finding my newer and longer books sell better at higher prices. I still price novellas, short novels and older books at 99 cents. Then releases from 2013 are $2.99. Releases from 2014 are $3.99, and $4.99 for my newest book.

Higher retail prices allow you to run really good specials on occasion.

If you have one book, publish it at $4.99 or higher. You want to see some money come in after all your hard work. Then you can run price specials for a week or run free days.

I advise against using $1.99 as a price. A Smashwords study showed that it sold fewer books than any other price by a long shot.

If you have several books, use different price points. Tempt readers with a free book, free days, a 99 cents book, and some at $2.99. These should be your loss leaders to your more expensive books.

If you have five or more books, start new books over $4.99. Again, you can run specials and free days, but your goal should be to start getting your overall average profit per book higher.

If you have a series, price the first one the lowest to draw people in. You can put out new books at a higher price or run them all cheap and have a box set.

Just a note: If you price your books at $2.99 and enroll in Kindle Select, you can get borrows that seem to run an average of $1.30, as of this writing in December 2014 . So if you price your books higher, you might get more borrows (because they're saving money) but you'll actually lose money instead of gaining. Of course you'll make more per *sale* at prices over $2.99.

There are other pricing strategies. You can lower the price and run a big promotion, such as Bookbub or other paid advertising. Once sales get going, raise the price to $2.99 or higher.

2015 Note:

During 2014, the big publishers in the US lowered book prices following a lawsuit about ebook price setting. Before, the big publishers had higher ebook prices and Indie authors were able to under sell them. That's not the case in the US anymore, with ebook prices leveling out.

In other countries, many people seem to think a cheap book can't be any good. So I advise to use standard ebook prices so that your ebook is around the same price as other books in your genre around the same length. Of course, you can then put them on special for a limited time.

Audio Books

I had a great run with audiobooks during 2013. That changed in 2014 when Kindle Unlimited allowed readers to get the audiobooks using the program. As of 2015, I'm still excited about audiobooks and plan to publish more, but for now I'm waiting for the market to change.

Authors in the US can use www.acx.com to collaborate with a narrator for free. It's a great service. Some authors are still choosing to find and hire a narrator on their own and producing their own audiobooks.

I'm hearing that authors in other countries don't have the same access. Also, because I'm not perusing this right now, I'll keep this section short. There are numerous articles and blogs out there on audiobooks already.

Translations

Translations are another way to multiple your income streams from your books. I always jump on new opportunities, which often allows me to make money on it before it changes or becomes too competitive. Audiobooks is one example. I think that will come back around in the future. For now, I'm focusing on translating my work into different languages.

Ebook markets around the world are developing and growing, so this is a great opportunity in my mind. I had one Spanish translation before 2014, and then Amazon Crossing translated one of my novels into German. That was released in October and has been selling well. During 2014, I learned about Babelcube and waited a few months to see how it went for other authors. I decided to go for it, and now I have seven published translations with several more in the works.

There are many ways to go about translating your work. I hired a translator for my first translation. He was a friend who happened to be highly qualified as a translator and court interpreter. Many translators will work for an upfront fee, or a fee and royalties. When hiring someone privately, you want to ensure that either they will handle editing and proof reading, or you plan to take care of it.

You may speak two languages so you can be involved in the translation, or know people who can help. It's fairly easy to find and hire an editor through a freelance site. I use Guru.com and Elance.com which both have projects posted for translation. I'm sure there are many other sites and translating services.

Babelcube.com allows you to create a profile and post books, and then translators make offers to translate. There's no upfront cost to the author. The translator is paid through royalties, and he/she gets the majority share at first. The royalty structure favors the translator and slowly shifts to favor the author to ensure the translator is compensated. I've enjoyed working with translators from German, Argentina, Spain, Italy and Portugal. This partnership also means I have someone promoting the book in their country and language.

To make an offer, a translator delivers a small sample. You can hire someone else to check this if you don't know anyone who speaks the given language.

I've focused on thinking globally over the last year because ebooks sell around the world and I can even translate work into other languages. "Thinking Globally" means translating work and including international links on my website. I'm thrilled that people can read my work in other languages, and it increases my product line at the same time.

Part 3: Strategies to Increase Sales

I love reading about how people succeed in general, and especially how authors make it. Many of the "instant" Indie successes weren't sure how they did it. They published a book and watched sales grow quickly, sometimes with some paid or free marketing or sometimes without any. In those cases, with or without a marketing campaign, I think we can agree for the most part that they had a special book.

That leads to a simple strategy: just keep writing. Maybe the tenth book you publish will go huge, and then your backlist will sell like crazy too. Or maybe you'll steadily grow a readership until you have so many books, and so many readers, that the numbers add up and push you over the top.

The following are ways to reach readers, sell more books, and grow a readership.

The Winning Mix

This has been my guiding strategy all along:

1. Produce a great story
2. Have a great cover, title, and description
3. Have a positive author personality
4. Have a continual online presence

This sounds overly simplistic, obvious, and easy, and I suppose it is. Still, this sums up much of what I say in this book and it keeps me on track. It reminds me to always work on my writing and storytelling, produce a professional book based on what works, be positive and fun online, and stay in touch with readers. I can break it down a bit more:

1. Readers want high drama, emotionally torn characters, conflict, growth and a great ending. I try to learn from reviews and reader feedback through emails and comments, and then write stories that are clicking with my readers.
2. I talked about book covers, titles, and description in the publishing section. You can hire people to help you with your book's package, and you can test titles, covers, and descriptions with your online networks and fans on your Facebook page. Readers seem to love being involved in the writing and publishing process these days. I'll ask for help on a story question, naming a character, which cover is better, which title, etc. It can really engage people in your writing.
3. I guess I just covered this one in #2. You don't have to push your books constantly to be talking about them.
4. By "continual online presence," I don't mean you need to be on Facebook or Twitter all day. You do need to write or maybe work at your day job.

However, you can put in a little time here and there, on a continual basis.

How do these really work together? When your book starts selling, or gets a bump in ranking or sales, it appears that Amazon will promote your book more. Many people call this traction. If you get sales going, the book and Amazon sustain them. However, when reader attention wanes, so does this selling mechanism.

I've also noticed that there are certain milestones, or steps, that you can pass in book sales which help pick up speed. It seems to work like this: the more you sell, the more Amazon promotes your book. If you sell, say, 100 a month, then 500, and then 1000, it shows that your book is selling more and more due to the writing, its package, and word of mouth.

Using Free Books to Sell Books

I've given away a million books and counting through Kindle Select free days and permafree books. (Explained soon.) I have no idea how many more I've given away through other ebook retailers and piracy sites. You see, I'm all for giving away books. I've seen, over and over, that giving away books leads to more book sales. (Think of how many people discover an author through the public library or from a friend who loaned them a book.)

The point of putting a free book out there is to let readers try your writing style and your brand. Free books are not as effective as they once were for a bump in sales, but they are still valuable as a promotion tool.

Tips:
* Make sure your free read is as polished as your other work.
* Try this when you have at least five other books so people can buy your work if they like your style.
* Make the first in a series free to draw readers in.
* It's a great promotional tool when you can tell potential readers: Try my work for free before you buy!
* Think of this as a long term strategy to build your reader base.
* Free stories are a great way to thank your current readers.

I like to make one of my novels or novellas perma-free through Smashwords for several months, and then I change to a different book. I simply change the first book back to the original price and mark another book free.

How to make ebooks free

You can publish a book on Smashwords and mark it free, and it will distribute to all the other ebook sites for free as well. Kindle will price match your book and make it free there too.

On Babelcube, you can make a book permanently free or run a promotion. The site has instructions. For perma-free, you need to do this when you publish, and it remains free. The promotions are on a tab on your translations page.

The Juggling Strategy

Have you ever watched someone juggle? It can be a bit hypnotizing to watch the balls fly up into the air in rhythm. As funny as this sounds, I use this idea in my book marketing. Let me explain:

Readers don't like to get hit with the same promotional posts all the time. Even if you keep your promotional Facebook posts to under 10%, you still don't want to push the same book every time. Ditto on Twitter. So, if you have several books, you can promote one and get sales going, and then move to the next. Imagine books flying up, one after another.

You might not be reaching the same people every time, but even then it helps you to rotate through your books. I'll rotate for a while and then I'll run a promotion with a bunch of my books as part of the rotation.

You can do this with paid promotions and freebies. I have enough ebooks that I can run freebies almost every weekend, if I plan it out. That's one way to juggle. I don't want to burn people out on the freebie idea either, so I often run a book free for all five days to get the maximum benefit. If I do it that way, I can run a freebie every couple of weeks with a different book.

With this strategy, even if one book is slipping, another is going up. Sometimes a promotion will work very well and send a book way up. The higher sales then ripple out in my other books.

How this idea can help you:
* When sales slow for your most recent book or the one you've been pushing, switch to another.
* If you've paid for a promotion with a site, you'll need to use another book if you run another promotion within their time frames.
* Rotating through your books will help you touch a wider variety of readers.

* If you promote one of your books at a time instead of all of them, it will send that one book up higher. It'll get a higher ranking and reach more people than if you diluted the promotion across several books. The bigger success of that one book will in turn spark second-book sales, so you end up with more sales.

Novellas

Back before the ebook boom, publishers had word count rules for each imprint. Each romance line had a very tight window and wouldn't even consider books outside that word count. There has also been an expectation that novels need to be a certain length for the given genre. Genre word counts still hold, but not as rigidly.

There are many readers that like ebooks because they can find shorter books to read. If you're reading on an Iphone at the doctor's or coffee shop, it's nice to find a fun little novella. In reality, freedom to publish a work of any length opens a door wide to opportunities.

Don't worry that readers will rate a novella lower simply because it's shorter. It's not the length that matters. It's all about how well the story is developed. I've seen this over and over. If a novella is a great read, it'll get good reviews. If it seems like you simply didn't want to finish a novel, readers will notice and say so in a review. My novellas are rated about the same as my novels.

I've had great success selling Christmas novellas for 99 cents. Ebook prices are going up right now—Amazon favors higher priced books whereas we could drive sales with 99 cent books before. So, it stands to reason that we can price our novels higher and write shorter books for the lower price ranges.

One important note: Amazon is now removing ebooks under 2500 words. A good novella length, in my mind, is at least 10,000 words. I think the very short ebooks came from people who were putting up nonfiction articles such as how to, self help, and the like.

Benefits of Novellas:
* You can write and publish many more per year, getting more books to put free and more books to be borrowed.
* You can use a novella for your perma-free book.

* You can write a series with a theme and then make a box set.
* You can price them lower so more people will be willing to pay for them.
* You have more books out there to be discovered. Each book is another point of visibility.
* You can improve your story craft in leaps and bounds with each new story you write. A novella is shorter, true, but you still have to develop characters and a great plot. With a shorter work, it seems like you can focus on craft even more, and have more confidence because it's easier to wrap your brain around the entire work, at least in my experience.

Possible Benefits:

Some authors test a market or idea with a novella—just be careful. I think they work best when they strengthen your overall brand. Of course, if your novels haven't been selling as you hoped, a novella in a new genre might open doors.

Novellas work well:
* If you clearly mark them as a shorter work so readers don't feel ripped off
* If they're a complete story
* If they have a crisis or problem that is solved
* Are written with the same quality as your novels
* As a new release between novels
* To keep readers interested
* To generate buzz
* To fill in gaps in a series
* To fill out side character's stories

I've seen some authors publish a prologue or teaser to an upcoming novel as a novella, with mixed results. This idea works if you have a good, full story, and not just a preview to market the full novel—see below.

Box Sets

After mentioning box sets so often, I should cover them in more detail. Normally you put a series in a box set, with a table of contents so readers can move around to different novels. You just highlight each book title and mark it as Heading 1, and then insert a Table of Contents at the beginning. You'll also want to mark the table of Contents as such: put your curser in front the word Contents (or Table of Contents), click insert Bookmark, and type, TOC. That way, Kindle will recognize it as the menu.

You can use a box set for a series, a theme or just related books. I have my first four romances in a box set. I have plans for more box sets in the future with a Christmas theme, and sets with different series in them, once I have more books in my series.

In general, I haven't seen box sets priced very high. Mine is currently priced $4.99. It has to be a really good deal for readers to take a bigger risk and buy several of your books at once. Even if they're ready to make that commitment, anything priced at 6.99 or higher just sounds high in the Kindle market.

Having a box set in Kindle Select gives you another title to put free. Of course, you'll only get around $2 for borrows, but you'll be getting new readers. I want all the points of visibility I can get in the Kindle store, so I'm all for box sets.

For the cover, many authors have a designer make a picture of the spines so it actually looks like a box set in a store. I had my four covers put together, facing out, which worked well with four books.

Another nice thing about sets: the books are already edited and proofed, so you don't have additional production costs.

Tips:
* Ensure the books are related enough that they'll all interest the same readers. Mine are romance and romantic suspense, but I wouldn't group together very different genres.

* Romance readers usually prefer a certain level of sensuality. You wouldn't want a sweet romance with erotica. (You probably don't want a huge sensuality range across your author brand, for that matter.)
* Keep the included books for sale separately.
* Have something outside of the box set for readers to buy if you can.
* Remember, if you need to update one of the books, update the box set too.

Write Like the Wind!

So you've probably noticed by now that having multiple books gives you a huge edge through:
* More points of visibility
* More books to put free
* More books to be borrowed
* More stories to talk about online
* More books for new readers to buy
* More stories to interest and attract different readers
* More books in the "also bought" section (see next section)
* Possibly your books appearing in the "bought instead" section at the bottom of the page
* A bigger resume
* Proof that you can write
* Proof that you're in it for the long haul
* Your style and author brand

I had a "wow" moment this year when I looked through my reviews. Readers were talking about their favorite Kristen James book, or mentioned that they didn't like a certain one as much, or said they've read many of my books. I already knew people were reading multiple books (because my 'Also Bought' sections are often full of my own books) but this really brought it home. I get emails and comments from readers that just found me or they wanted to tell me they've read all of my romances. I thought I'd share a post from Facebook that makes a very good point about multiple books and visibility:

"Just finished reading *More than Memories* and can't wait for the sequel. I also didn't realize I actually have a few of your other books. I didn't realize I had a few of them and even left feedback on two! I have loved all your books so far. Thank you! I have enjoyed them."

This isn't the first time that someone wrote me to say they loved a book, and then realized they had a few of my books already on their Kindle from a free promotion. So they went back and read all of them.

This is a new kind of visibility: *already* being on someone's Kindle when they realize they love your writing.

I've hinted at it all through this book: it takes a while to write and publish several books, but it's well worth it. When sales are down and you want to take to Facebook and promote, remember to keep writing. In fact, maybe it's better to focus that energy more into writing than all the work we can do online.

Write a Series

Many authors love to write in series. It helps you by providing the characters, possibly the setting, and all or some of the back story. A series can be developed by continuing the characters' storylines on another adventure, using secondary characters, or even just using the same setting. Romance readers enjoy books all set in the same little town. Series are a great way to pull readers in.

Write a Related Book

A related book might use the same setting or a character, but not be an exact sequel. Here's how I did it:

I have *Embers of Hope* and *More Than a Promise* in my Second Gift Series. However, *More Than a Promise* is set at Ocean View Stables from *A Cowboy for Christmas*.

It made the writing even more fun for me—I got to revisit the stables along with Missy and Brent from that story.

I'm not the only author using this. J.A. Konrath recently released a book called Haunted House. His blog talks about how it's the sequel to six other unrelated books.

(See www.jakonrath.blogspot.com/2013/05/haunted-house.html)

Having multiple books really draws readers in—if they love your style, they'll most likely read their way through all your books. Now imagine if, on top of that, your stories are related. This strategy really shines in the "Customers Also Bought" section, which is my next tip.

"Customers Also Bought"

This isn't exactly a strategy, but it's a way to know if readers are coming back for a second book—if the "Customers Also Bought" section shows your other books.

The "Also Bought" section on your book's page works in many different ways to help you. At first glance, you might not think so. It's a way for Amazon to promote other books, in case readers decide they're not interested in your book. Yes, that means you can have book competition right there on your own book page, from books that are similar to yours.

You *want* this section to be full on your book's page. That might seem counterintuitive since it's advertising other books, but it shows that a lot of people have also bought your book. It shows that you're selling. When you put your book for free and get a lot of downloads, it helps to fill up this section.

You can also do a little market research here. What books are selling with yours? Are they priced higher or the same? How many reviews do they have? If you see an author showing up again and again, that means you're competing in the same category. Check out their website and what they're doing. If you see someone that is also a part of your social networks, you may consider doing some cross promoting and helping each other. It doesn't hurt you. Readers are always looking for new books and it's not like someone will steal your customer. That customer can read books by both of you!

The "Also Boughts" are also advertising your book on other books' pages, so it's a good thing. The more your book sells, the more it shows up in this little section, which is another reason to have a cover that looks great when it's small.

In the best case scenario, you'll see a bunch of your own books in there. That tells you that readers are buying more than one of your books. That means they read one book and liked it enough to read more—congrats!

This is why it's good to promote your backlist and not just your newest release. I promote one book, give it a bump in ranking and sales, and move on to the next. I try to keep bumping different books because they promote each other.

You can use the front and end matter of your book to promote all of your work. Keep older books on your website too. Everything really does add up, and you'll see your books showing up together on Amazon and readers talking about them.

Email List

Many authors say this is the most important aspect of their marketing efforts. If the idea of "email list" confuses you, it's also called a newsletter. I held off on starting one for the last several years—I reasoned that people could stay up to date with my updates through Facebook, Twitter, and my blog. (People can already subscribe to my blog.) I thought I might have too many links at the end of my books with all the different social sites. I also knew, though, that different people like to connect in different ways. Some people love Twitter and won't follow you on Facebook. There are also people who prefer a newsletter.

There's another important reason to have an email list: so you can let everyone know about your new book. People can miss an update on Facebook and Twitter. With an email list, you have access to the emails, which you don't get when people subscribe to your blog.

I use www.Mailchimp.com, which lets you start a free email list when you start. You only pay when you reach a certain number of subscribers. I've included the link to my signup page at the back of my books and on my Facebook Page Note called book links.

I have a bad habit of subscribing to things and then not opening the newsletters. The big reason is I get so many from the same person. I think most people are busy and don't want to open a newsletter every day, week or even month. Newsletters are great for rounding up information, so you can send one out monthly or even less often, to:

* Announce new releases
* Share exciting news such as a big milestone
* Talk about your work in progress
* Announce soon-to-be released books, novellas, etc
* Share contests, specials, and freebies

A good newsletter will have new information, some personal touches, and several things that your readers will find valuable. Have a hook, like you would with a book, so people have a reason to open the letter, and then share enough different things to keep it interesting.

In the best-case scenario, you'll be growing your reader base. When you release a book that people are waiting for, they'll buy your book. It's the most reliable way to let readers know what is going on.

Your Marketing Plan

There's some advice I hear so often I tune it out: Write a marketing plan! Follow everyone on Twitter! Do a huge book launch!

Well, writing a marketing plan is a good idea. I keep a running marketing plan on my desktop that I update with new steps for each month, along with my overall goals and ideas. I tend to be a bit lax about things, so most people want something more structured. A good marketing plan should list all the steps you can reasonably take and a timeline.

For a book launch, I recommend staggering your steps. Don't try to do everything the first day or week. When I'm not launching a book, I've even keep it as simple as trying to do one promotional thing a day.

Spreading your efforts out to a daily effort helps keep you sane and it helps steadily build your online presence. It even helps your book ranking. Here's two simple lists to start with:

Launching a Book:
* Budget money for advertising
* Budget time for looking up reviewers and submitting your book
* Budget time for researching marketing (such as reading this book and reading online blogs and articles. I've listed quite a few resources.)

In Between Book Launches:
* Budget time to write
* Time for blogging and posting on your Facebook page and Twitter
* Keep track of promotions and results, both to improve what you do and time future promotions.

I've kept these simple for a very important reason. In my experience, and I've seen this repeated by other authors, the things that help sell books are, in order of effectiveness:

* Creating a great story and package
* Freebies
* Building an audience on a Facebook page (see next section)

How to Use Social Networking

The easy advice is: use social networking to network socially, NOT to become a monotone about your book(s).

Networking might even be the wrong word. It makes me think of business professionals working their contacts for their own gain. As authors, we're "friend-connecting." People find us either through reading our work or seeing a shared post or promotion online, and then they check out our page. Liking a Facebook page is a small commitment, in a way. These people thought they'd find value in our posts. So they're not there to hear about every review (since they probably read the book) or every time you rank in a category. Since fans are making a commitment, I think we should make a commitment to act like a friend, not a book seller.

Once you have a book out there, it's time to create a fan page on Facebook so readers can like your page. (Not a page for each book. It'll drive you nuts, and people don't want to like five different pages.) This gives you a public space where you can talk about your books and writing, have giveaways, announce new books and freebie days, and connect with readers. I know some authors use their personal profile, but you will probably want to keep them separate, especially if you plan on having a lot of fans. This way, your non book friends can still be your friend on your personal profile.

I launched my FB author page when I decided to get serious about selling ebooks. Sales began climbing that month and have grown ever since.

I post almost daily and check my favorite pages pretty often too. I've used my author page to like all kinds of book blogger pages and publishing professionals, so Facebook keeps me up to date on what's going on in the reading world. With recent changes, pages can receive and send messages too. You can check out my author page and what I'm doing at: www.Facebook.com/WriterKristenJames.

I have my Facebook linked to my Twitter account so that my FB posts go onto Twitter. (To do this: log on as your page, look under Edit Page, and then resources.) You can do this through Hootsuite too, and have that site post to all your social networking sites. That seems a bit impersonal to me, but I do like linking the two sites I use the most.

Guideline #1, across all networks, is to use your face and not your book cover. People like to connect with a person on Facebook and Twitter, not a book cover.

Guideline #2 – be a fun person! Be interesting and intriguing, and tell us about more than your book and your reviews. While experimenting the first six months, I realized that it hurts sales to push your books hard. If you back off with the promotion and just be a fun, interesting person, people want to talk about your books more. Sales go up. Fans like to hear about the writing life and everything else that you're passionate about.

Guideline #3 – Use your social sites to announce new books and giveaways/contests/raffles, but strive to keep your promotional posts to 10% or less. If you're a fun, interesting person, readers will check out your books. Note: talking about writing isn't pushing your books, and people enjoy knowing what you're working on. Many people like your page because they enjoyed your book, so you don't have to beat your fans over the head with, "Check out my newest review!"

Guideline #4 – Get involved with book bloggers, readers, reading groups and discussions as a person, not just an author or your brand. Be real.

Tip: Hard promoting annoys readers. Help people, offer advice, join discussions, and be yourself online. People know you're an author and will click your links.

Facebook Insights
The top of your FB page has a small box labeled "Insights." When you click "see all," you can open several pages of very useful information about people who like your page, by city, country, sex, and age. I found it interesting that most of my likes come from women in three age groups that span age 25 up to 54. However, the most engagement and

interaction comes from women ages 45 to 54. That does make a difference in how what I post about.

The Insights also show you when people like and unlike your page, which is one way to track how you attract and run off fans. It's normal to see likes all the time and unlikes here and there, sometimes one or two a day. These come from people who might like your page, look around, and then realize it's not for them. That's okay. But if you get five or more unlikes on the same day, take a look at what you posted. This is how to tell if you're promoting too much.

At the top of the page, you'll see a box with all your posts and how many people you reached. You can combine this with the likes and comments on a post to see what clicks with your fans.

More Tips to Engage Fans:
* Use conversational posts on Facebook instead of marketing.
* Photos really engage people—they're more eye grabbing in the timeline. I get a ton of interaction on book related photos.
* Fans love to hear about your work in progress and future books—these kinds of posts are the most popular on my page.
* Post questions to get to know people.

Twitter

What I share here is my personal preference, but it's something that might help you. I'm admitting I have some weird ideas…

Every author on Twitter begins their little bio with "Author of…" I started mine with something about me and then added that I write books. It drives me nuts that so many people follow me simply because we're both authors. I don't think they plan to actually interact with me—they're building their numbers. Most people are fine with this, and will follow a fellow author back. I follow back when the bio sounds interesting, and doesn't begin with, "Author of..." (I warned you that I have different ideas on this!)

But think about it, do readers want to follow you back simply because you're an author they've never heard about? Even if you're in the genre they read? And does connecting with every other author on Twitter help us? It might if we're talking and sharing information and encouragement, but that hasn't been the case for me on Twitter. Instead, if I follow an author back, I begin seeing tweets about their reviews, books, sales, and how I should go get the book.

These days, it seems that everyone and their mother is publishing a book, so it just makes you fade into all the static to have that be your main feature.

So my advice for Twitter is to have a unique bio that tells something about you outside of being a writer—perhaps your subject matter, your passion or something that will help you connect to other people.

Here's my Twitter bio:

"Adventure seeker who loves the outdoors & exploring. I write romances with dreamy men and strong women."

My location is "On the river, Oregon."

This way, I hope to connect with people that love the outdoors, and possibly reading romances.

I also uploaded a background that showcases my book covers. If someone sees one of my tweets, or visits my profile after reading my book or seeing me online, they'll see my covers and web address.

There are many fun and creative ways to connect with new people on Twitter, or any social site, by posting about things outside of writing and promoting. Right now I have a profile picture with actor/singer Christian Kane, which helped me connect with an entirely different audience than my romance readers. There are some Kaniacs that followed me on Twitter and Facebook, and they're among my frequent commenters. That's just one way of creating some buzz, which gets your name and books in front of new people. You can do something similar by joining a literary event or even promoting a national event or charity that's donating books or raising money. Sharing life events can interest people who might not normally take a look at your books, but after connecting with you on a different level, they'll be more interested. This includes celebrating and promoting other authors. If you share what you're reading, it gives people even more insight to what your books might be like. Plus, as authors, it's fun for us to talk about books!

How to Use Your Website or Blog

It's not a question of having a site or not. It's easy and even free to have a website, and it puts all of your writing information in one place.

If readers come to your website or blog, they want to learn more about you and your books. This is the place to show off your personality and passion, not only for writing, but for reading and other hobbies. It's also the place where you can do all the promoting I said not to do on Facebook. Include your best reviews, awards, honors, previews, and tiny teasers.

Many authors think of their website or blog as their home base. It's the first thing they start online and their central location in a way. When readers find one of your books and like it, it's the place they go to for more information. Whether you have a website or a blog, you can include links for people to like you on Facebook and follow you on Twitter. If you have a blog, people can subscribe via email so they'll know when you write a new post.

Blog or Website?

This is a matter of personal preference, and the two options are not exclusive of each other. Here's a few of the options out there:

Professionally designed websites – these look very nice but you may or may not have the option to update often.

Self-designed website – you can design these in a program and you will likely have the freedom to update regularly. Yahoo offers webhosting and it's easy to sign up. You can create your site from scratch or use a template. If you've ever used a card designing program or edited photos, you can probably design a basic website.

Website with a blog – for a while, I used a Yahoo website and had a page that linked to my blog so that it showed up on the site. There's other ways to do this, especially if you work with a web designer.

Blog – there are several blog hosts out there. Wordpress and Blogger are the biggest. I wasn't happy with my website/blog set up, so I tried Blogger. I quickly moved over to Wordpress.

I love Wordpress and have used it for several years. Here's some of the features:

* You can pick a template and customize the color theme and layout.
* You can add pages and subpages.
* You can add widgets so things show up on the side of your blog.
* You can add your own header photo.
* You can buy a custom web address for under $20 a year.
* Web hits show up in Dashboard and you can click "View All" to see the number of visitors, how many pages those people viewed, what country they came from, what page referred them, what search engine referred them, most popular search terms, and most popular tags. These last two are especially helpful.

It's also more interactive and allows visitors to leave comments. And one last bonus, search engines love blogs.

A great way to use your website or blog is to provide readers with previews. This is how you hook them with your story and show you can write. Post the beginning of upcoming books. Once the book is published, post scenes from later chapters, since the Amazon preview shows the beginning.

Your website is a great central location for your promotions, too, and then you can advertise them across all your networks.

Tip: Take some time to check out the website and blogs of your favorite authors and other bestselling authors. Things change so quickly online that I have a feeling we'll be doing more and more with our websites in the future.

More tips:

* Have a site that doesn't take ten years to load. Don't have a bunch of moving graphics or changing picture boxes. One of these items is usually enough.
* People like simple layouts with 'white space' or room between different elements.
* Keep your site or blog easy to navigate.
* Most importantly, don't limit yourself. There is so much you can do with a website or blog. You might have endless ideas that I haven't thought about or tried. Look around online. Experiment.

What to Blog About

Many fiction authors wonder what on earth do they put on a blog. I've gone with my Oregon theme and blog about hiking, fishing, and other outdoor adventures, along with posts about what I'm writing and new releases or editions such as audio books or a Spanish version. You might have some hobbies you'd like to share and readers like learning about the people behind the books.

A blog is a great place to post a contest or giveaway. It's also fun to join a blog hop. I've found several that were posted on a Facebook page I liked. The host would have a blog topic, such as our favorite drink to have with a good book. We'd write a short blog and post the contest.

Reviews

A simple way to get more reviews is to kindly ask for them at the end of your book. You can insert a link to your book's page on Amazon to make it easy. (Of course, you have to publish the book to get the link but you can add it in and republish.)

Amazon asks people to rate the book at the end, but the rating doesn't actually go on Amazon—it posts to their social networks if they've connected any. (Which still helps you, but not with building up reviews on Amazon.) Of course, Amazon also emails people and asks them to review books on Amazon.

Free promotions are another way to build reviews quickly. All of these methods will bring in reader reviews.

Warning: Amazon deletes reviews if they suspect the reviewer has a personal relationship with the author, or was involved in any way in producing the book. That means it's not beneficial to ask friends and family to review your books. There are other triggers that will cause Amazon to delete reviews. A couple years ago I read several articles about Amazon developing a computer program that could search for fake reviews. It somehow uses key words and phrases in reviews. A study proved the program could spot fake reviews with great accuracy, while people can't. Apparently we fall for fake reviews for all kinds of merchandise.

Book Bloggers and Reviewers

As I've said, it's getting harder and harder to get reviews by submitting to book bloggers and reviewers. I still see people asking how to find reviewers, so here's to resources:

The Writer's Resource Directory
http://writersresourcedirectory.com/Book_Reviewers.html

The Best Book Reviewers on Twitter
http://www.mediabistro.com/galleycat/best-book-reviewers-on-twitter_b11136

Both of these sites have a long list of book reviewers and bloggers.

When you email them about a review or submit your information through their website, list your title, genre, word count, and an enticing book description.

Since the ebook explosion, book bloggers have become very busy people, so you'll need to befriend them online. Follow their blogs, their Twitter accounts, and like them on Facebook. Join their conversations. See what they like to read. Read and follow their guidelines. Support them too – promote their book page and blog and give them a shout out. They like getting fans too. Then, when you email about getting a book review, let them know that you follow and support them.

*On a side note, many book bloggers have a blog and a page on Facebook. They love to run blog hops and events. I've donated ebooks to many of these events because I saw someone post a request on Facebook for donations. Joining these doesn't take much time and it keeps you connected with book bloggers and readers, expands your network, and is a lot of fun.

Tip: Make a Word doc or spreadsheet on your computer and collect names and email addresses for book reviewers. I also write down their book blog address so I can double-check their guidelines before submitting. I record when I submitted and the results.

Goodreads

Just as you should create a profile on Author Central, you really should have one on Goodreads. Creating a profile allows you to add your books, your bio, and your blog so it shows up on Goodreads.

Goodreads is the biggest site out there when it comes to rating, reviewing, and talking about books. They add them to lists and shelves on their pages. Every time a reader rates or reviews a book, it goes onto their stream for their friends to see. It's instant word of mouth. And now that Amazon bought Goodreads, it'll become even more important.

You can actually buy advertising on Goodreads. I've done it a few times, but I recommend waiting until you've built up reviews.

Running free promotions is a great way to get reviews on both Amazon and Goodreads. So is a special price or a Bookbub promotion. Whenever I have a good sales run with a book, I get a rash of reviews on both sites.

Paid Advertising

You can find endless advertising opportunities online. It sometimes seems that a new opportunity pops up every day. In the last couple of years, there were a few really good sites that would run your book in a daily email, manage Facebook and Twitter posts, and offer a blog post. Some of these have loaded up so much that no one book sees any real benefit. I've stopped using all of them except two:

Bookbub – probably the most expensive, but it's the one that's getting results right now. This site has shot one of my books to the #2 spot in free three times now. It costs around $200 to advertise a free book and $400 for a 99 cents book. The price varies a bit by genre, and by how much the book costs. Interestingly, they charge the most for mystery and thrillers because that category has the most subscribers. It's followed by romance.

Ereader News Today – charges 25% of your profit from the sales that went through their sites. They use affiliate links so they know how many books they sell for you. That makes this one worthwhile. You only pay for what you actually get.

I've dabbled in other promotional opportunities in the last six months and found them lacking. Some are too new to show results, such as Authorgraph's new paid advertising. I tried it for a month and didn't notice any difference. Others have been around awhile and, I think, gotten too busy with book listing. They run twenty or more books a day. One site lists results, but when I compared my results with what they recorded, the results always looked better on the site.

I often get emails from new services offering to review my book, promote it on their page, or offer some other paid service. You really have to check into how popular their site is and if other authors have had positive results. Many of these paid services are either new or still too small. They don't seem to reach that many readers.

Facebook promotions – you can set your budget for each post you promote or boost on Facebook, with daily or lifetime budgets. You can click "Boost" right on the post, but that's not the best way to do it. It'll promote to everyone. If you go into the ads section, you can create a new ad that promotes a post, and you can select keywords, target audiences, and other factors that will target your audience much better.

Facebook promotions are easy to use and they're helpful for building likes on your page. Quite a few people find my page this way and then they'll grab one of my freebies. Soon they're reading all my books. I can't say that a Facebook promotion leads to direct sales the day I run it. I've run ads and boosted posts about a paid book, but the cost per click was higher than the profit I made on the book. I've often boosted posts about a free book, but they don't actually generate that many clicks to Amazon. The Facebook paid promotions work best for building my fan base, which does sell books in the long run.

I prefer using paid promotions over author liking groups, where a group of authors all like each other's pages. That might bring the numbers up a bit, but you want to reach readers.

A Few Warnings:

* Watch out for sites that sell reviews. I used one that said it'd send my book out to its community of reviewers and get at least 10 reviews. I think I ended up with three over a month and I'm not sure the reviewers were even in my target audience.
* Watch out for sites that email you. If you haven't heard of them, check them out carefully. I actually found Bookbub this way, when they had an open spot and ran my book for free. They emailed me but I still checked into them before signing up.

Pay to Play

I see so many page owners on Facebook complaining that FB keeps people from seeing their posts unless they pay to promote them. I agree and feel for book bloggers and reviewers, and other pages that aren't selling things. It stinks that they built an audience and now can't reach them.

However, for the rest of us, the people who are on Facebook to build a fan base so we can make money, we should expect to pay for advertising. That was the whole point of Facebook. Sure, they started a free site and sucked everyone in, but they always planned to monetize it. (And so is everyone online these days. It's all about creating the next big website so you can monetize it and make billions.)

Well, we as authors are on Facebook with author pages to make money. It's a process, of course. We're building an audience so they'll read our free content and then buy our future books, right? I understand people are angry because it was free to reach people on Facebook before, but in business, you gotta pay to play. Advertising has traditionally been expensive, and that's why you need to be smart about it. Haven't you talked to someone who sank a lot of money into Google Adwords, only to waste it? At the same time, other people made a lot of money by figuring it out.

It doesn't take much money per post to promote for big results. The big players are paying and building big audiences. If you want to reach large numbers of people, it's going to cost money. You can try gimmicks and tricks to reach people without paying, and they work to some extent. They work even better if you promote that post for ten bucks. Spending a few hundred dollars on Facebook ads per month can go a long way. It gets attention, builds your Facebook fan base, and actually does reach more people.

(Side note: posting interesting and fun posts once or twice a day keeps the page active. If you post every few days, far less people see your posts.)

There are other pay to play options out there, such as Bookbub, which seem expensive but do generate results. As your books earn more and more royalties, you can put a little aside into your marketing fund each month. If you plan for marketing expenses, and invest that money wisely, it can make all the difference.

Breaking Out

There are so many books out there that promise they can give you the secret to making millions on Kindle. But if any of those methods worked, wouldn't we all be millionaires?

The truth is, if you study all the Indie authors who break out and land in the headlines, they've essentially followed the steps in this book. They put in the time and work to produce a great story. Then they marketed.

Like me, you might have followed the recent story of Rachel Abbott who wrote *Only the Innocent* and hit #1 on the Kindle best-seller list. I've read tidbits here and there, but one article put it all together for us: "Self-Publishing Success Stories: The Anatomy of a Kindle Bestseller," by Mark Edwards.

http://www.thecreativepenn.com/2013/01/21/self-publishing-success-kindle-bestseller/

Like Abbot, Edwards has succeeded in selling ebooks. He used both his own experience and Abbot's to create a list that covers some of my tips: you need a great cover and description, reviews and hard work. He also added a marketing plan, which is a highly useful tool for many writers who succeed. Abbot used Twitter to reach readers and had planned her approach for getting reviews.

As I read this story and other success stories, I always notice that each author found what worked for them. It's just about impossible for any of us to spread ourselves thin enough to engage each and every social network, and follow all of the methods that have worked for other authors. You may be a Twitter person or, like me, perhaps you like Facebook better. What matters is that you find a place where you can connect with people.

There's another thing I notice about huge success stories. The book itself generates buzz—everyone tells their friends about it. That goes back to the writing. So, as your promote your current books, keep learning and keep writing!

Here's a few honest and blunt tips about breaking out:

* When you're frustrated, keep moving. Don't stick to the same writing and promoting if it's not working. I give each book six months to see if sales grow. If not, I leave them be and take them out of my promotion rotation.
* Watch your reviews and those little pull outs next to the rating box. Are you getting good feedback? Can you learn from it?
* Read and study bestsellers. Think about gut emotional response. The big sellers aren't 'nice stories with good writing.' They aren't even about mostly good people with happy endings. The characters are likable but highly flawed, and they face tough dilemmas and decisions. To really break out, you need deep characters facing overwhelming problems.
* Writing a highly unique character and storyline makes it more universal.
* Don't edit out the things that feel too personal or revealing, or even too ugly.
* Remember this all takes time. We have some bestselling authors that published their first book and had 50,000 sales within a few months. They're in the news because it's so exciting. Yes, there are more and more stories like this, but there are even more midlist Indie authors that are making $4,000, $5,000 and even more a month without getting featured in national headlines. These authors are growing a readership in their genre, and they're developing an author brand. These authors often take off by sheer force of numbers.

The last element of achieving success in publishing is simple: you need good old fashioned timing and a bit of luck. Success stories from every industry show us the importance of luck. Whether it is a chance encounter, a phone call, a meeting, an online mention or review, or a connection. Don't let this get you down, though, because you can have one of those lucky moments at any time. (I've gotten reviews from Top 100 and Top 500 Amazon reviews through free days.) People who "get lucky" do so by having their books out there, doing interviews, writing blogs, and making connections. Be prepared to get lucky. You can't catch a fly ball if you're not looking for one.

I've had many moments when I stopped and suddenly realized, oh my gosh, I'm here, right where I wanted to be a year ago. I can get caught up in my goals and looking forward, so it can catch me by surprise when I look over my goals and realize I've reached them. I set a goal before, and now I'm working from home as a full-time author. I have to make new and bigger goals!

Final Tips:

* Network with other authors to share knowledge and experience. Network to make personal connections, too. It's not really helpful to anyone to push your book on other authors—instead, see authors as your co-workers and people who understand what you're going through.
* Hard selling pushes readers away. Seems like a catch-22, but I saw my sales take off when I put myself out there as a friendly person.
* Build on momentum! When sales take off, they can drop again. You might make ten grand in a month or reach a point where you think, "I've made it!" But if you don't keep an online presence, and pay for some advertising, sales can drop off again. Even if you start making good money with one book, keep writing to keep things going.
* Keep a journal to track your goals and progress. I use one big book to take notes on writing books and articles, and to write down my promotions and results. It's a record of my writing and publishing journey, so I

can go back and see my progress, see what works, and see what I'm learning about writing.

* Define success your way and celebrate milestones.
* Giant bestsellers have something "sticky" about the story—people keep thinking about it after they read it and they tell their friends. It's all about the story. If you keep writing, you'll write a book that clicks. Many big name traditional authors had several published books before they broke out of midlist.
* Finally, remember to keep the passion in your life and writing. Write stories that you *have* to write, that move you, that make you feel like you've written a masterpiece.

Selling a Self Published Book

Many authors want to know if it's possible to self publish a book and then sell it to a traditional publisher. The old fear was that once you published it yourself, no one would touch it. That thinking is very outdated! Many Indie authors are selling a self published book, a new book after self publishing, or part of their rights, such as just their print, audiobook or foreign rights. Anything is possible these days. If you can prove you can sell, you can write your own ticket.

I published *Point Hope* in conjunction with Zulu Productions in June, 2013. The first two weeks were quiet, sales wise, with just a few hundred sales. Then it took off, getting reviews and selling five thousand copies in a matter of weeks. That's not actually a mind-blowing number when compared to many books out there. It didn't even hit the top 100 in Kindle. But it did catch the attention of an editor with Montlake Romance, an Amazon Imprint. I was leaving the gym one night and saw an email. I almost deleted it because I get so many that try to sell me some of service. Then I noticed the publisher name in the email preview and opened it. After about a week's discussion, an offer came, and then Montlake acquired the book and relaunched it in October.

I think that's the typical way it happens, although some authors might query publishers about their self published book, with sales numbers included.

I've read many similar accounts and seen authors I know through Facebook get picked up by a publisher. In fact, some authors self publish as a part of their plan to reach a traditional publishing deal. I've lost count of the number of authors that are going both routes: working with a publisher on some deals while self publishing some of their books.

Of course there are authors turning down offers from publishers because they'd rather continue to self publish. I have to agree I love the creative freedom, the control, and the speed of self publishing. I'm especially excited that authors have to many options now.

Should You Sell?

Some authors advise not to sell your rights unless the advance is so big, you're happy even if that's all the money you get out of the deal. That's one way to look at it. There are other factors, too. I wanted to try it at least once. Why not? I could argue about whether I'll make more money or lose money, but I know I'll write many more books. So I took a gamble on Amazon Publishing. If I look at all of my book as my portfolio, it's a pretty cool credential. I'm sure it'll help me sell more copies, both from that book and my other books even if I self publish them.

It's a personal decision based on what you want, the offer, what's in the contract, and your goals.

Bonus Content

2.5 Years, 20 books, and 100k sales later—What I've Learned

Originally published on my website in December 2013

I often read the advice to stop checking sales, ranks, reviews, web hits, and focus on writing. It's some of the best advice out there, and advice I try to follow. On the other hand, sometimes it's healthy to pause and evaluate how you're doing. (Seems to be a trend at the end of the year!) It can also show you that you really have built something.

I have 10 novels, 7 novellas and 3 nonfiction books, and reached 1,000 reviews on Amazon this month. I don't think it's bad to check in on sales and reviews, if you keep it under control. I used to read reviews and see if I could learn anything from them--and reviews used to be longer and more detailed. I often get short reviews these days, especially for my novellas. Still, I like to glance through once in a while to see what readers are saying. Amazon Central puts them all in one place so it's easy. It's fine to have good and bad reviews; it shows that your book is selling.

On ranking: I used to check my book ranks, but now I mainly check the rank for my most recent book, or a book that I'm running a promotion on. I look at my author rank in Author Central to see the overall trend. (But in general, I'm trying to check less and write more.)

On predicting: I've had some awesome months when I had a new release or a promotion went really well, but I've learned that I can't take that and make a monthly prediction of steady growth. Sales go up and down. I put my sales into Excel and then create a month by month chart showing book sales and income. I have another chart that shows yearly book sales and income, so I can see the upward progress every year. It's the big picture that matters.

On Changing Amazon: In 2011 and 12, it seemed most of my books would sell and have different seasons and spikes. Since this summer, however, it seems Amazon promotes new books, giving them a chance to succeed at first, but sales for my older books have slowed down. (That follows a more traditional model than what I've seen on Amazon since 2011, and it might change again in a few months.)

On crazy ebook growth in 2012--there were some blockbuster books the last couple of years that really drove sales. That can happen again. A book or series will come out that will be different, and it'll see sales like 50 Shades, Twilight, Hunger Games, Wimpy Kid and Wool. There's been huge bestsellers from both traditional and author published books.

That naturally leads into my next observation: things change constantly. In the last two years, we've had all kinds of storms. The huge ebook growth, then people crying that the sky was falling, then people saying Indie stores are making a comeback, and even times when people said books are on the way out. I know better than that one. But things do change, and they don't follow our predictions. The steady reality is that we keep getting surprised. I just have to focus on improving my writing. (I've been working on bigger story lines and deeper themes.)

Another change: I had a sales curve every year that dipped in the summer, but this last summer was more like my typical Decembers. I released a book that I really believed in, but I was surprised at how well it did. Of course, releasing new books has always been the best promotion, and I regret that I didn't have another one ready to release this fall or winter. Montlake Romance re-released Point Hope in late October, and I relied on that as my 'new book.' My next book is coming out in January, and I plan to write and publish 3-5 books this coming year.

With all the changes on Amazon, the US book market, and publishing in general, I'm going to expand into other retailers with some of my books. I'm very pro Amazon and feel extremely thankful to the company for opening the door to so many authors. I've built an audience and got a traditional publishing deal for one of my books that I published through Kindle. Because it's about my readers and reaching more readers, so I'm going to experiment with other retailers.

My biggest lesson: many of the promotional activities we're encouraged to do don't get the results we want. I used to advise people to build their "snowball," and I still believe in this idea, but there is also a 20/80 rule. 20% of what we do will get 80% of the results. In terms that I understand better, focus on the things that make big results. I experiment, and learn from other authors, and I focus on writing. Maybe I'm stating the same lesson over and over! It's about the writing. When I launch a book now, I basically publish it and post it here, on my FB page and Twitter. I also did a Goodreads giveaway with Point Hope and plan to do more of those.

The big things I've learned pertain to writing and storytelling, which of course is the whole point of all of this. I write, read novels, read books on writing, learn from podcasts and videos, write some more, repeat... and it's thrilling, challenging and fulfilling. I'm putting together a workbook on novel writing for a class I'm going to teach this coming year. I'm really excited about it. I keep files on everything I learn about writing, and now I get to put it all together with diagrams. :) I had some huge breakthroughs in structure this year, especially about how to up the tension and drama in a novel's middle, and I'm eager to share that. I'm going to publish the book so people who aren't local to take the class can also buy it.

One thing I keep in mind is that learning is a continuous, life long process. I have a thick journal where I record notes on useful writing books, videos, etc, and new things I learn. I write life posts and encouraging quotes too. It's a fantastic way to keep all my writing notes in one place, and I can look through it to refresh what I've learned. It's been one of the best things I've done for my writing career.

Also check out:

The Alliance of Independent Authors which runs a series called "How I Did It," featuring posts from many successful Indie authors. Here's my interview: How I Do It: Kristen James Shares The Secrets of Her Self-Publishing Success.

Writing and Publishing in 2015

The US ebook market has leveled in the last year in several ways:

Trade prices came down while some Indie prices have gone up, so there isn't the big gap that we saw before.

Before 2014, the ebook market favored Indie books because they had lower prices and could produce more books faster. Now things are leveling again so traditionally published authors and Indies are both offering qualities books are affordable prices.

Kindle Select gave Indie authors an edge but now it appears to hurt many by cutting their book sales and income.

Many Indie authors are finding success on other ebook retailers such as Barnes & Noble Nook, iTunes (iBooks), and Kobo.

Many readers have hundreds of unread books on their devices so they don't need more—it takes more value to get them to download even free books.

The good news is: authors are still breaking out. It takes hard work but that has been the case throughout history.

Globally, ebooks are catching on in many other markets. Those markets are enjoying some of the benefits we saw in the US three and two years ago.

All authors have an opportunity to sell around in the world in multiple languages.

Quality writing, great storylines, catching covers and titles are more important than ever to stand out.

In short, I feel authors must love storytelling and writing in order to have the dedication required for the long haul. Isn't that why we do this? I absolutely love sharing my stories and hearing from readers. I hope you've found this guide helpful, and I wish you great success in your writing and publishing journey.

Additional Resources with Links

"Self Publishing is the Future, and it's great for writers."
http://www.salon.com/2013/04/04/hugh_howey_self_publ
ishing_is_the_future_and_great_for_writers/

Articles by Elizabeth Sims on writing at
http://www.elizabethsims.com/short-works.php

Writer's Digest Second Draft Critique.
http://www.writersdigestshop.com/author-service-
center?lid=wdnav2nddraft

Quarterly short story contest at
http://www.nycmidnight.com/

"Ebook Formatting Fairies" April 12, 2013 post listing
real sales numbers for the last three years.
http://e-
bookformattingfairies.blogspot.com/2013/04/author-know-thy-
business-self.html

Alliance of Independent Authors
http://allianceindependentauthors.org/

Choosing A Self Publishing Service 2013: The Alliance of
Independent Authors Guide
http://amzn.com/B00CC0NYCM

The Creative Penn – Writing, Publishing, Marketing
www.thecreativepenn.com

Let's Get Digital blog (His books are *Let's Get Digital*
and *Let's Get Visible.)*
http://davidgaughran.wordpress.com/

Jane Friedman's blog. Writing, reading, and publishing in the digital age. http://janefriedman.com/

J.A. Konrath's blog about his writing and self publishing. He lists links for his print and ebook formatters, cover designer and other professional. He also shares his sales numbers and lot of opinion on the publishing industry. www.jakonrath.blogspot.com

Ebook Formatter
http://e-bookformattingfairies.blogspot.com/

Joanna Penn's list of recommended designers
http://www.thecreativepenn.com/bookcoverdesign/

A blog about watching out for assisted self publishers:
http://davidgaughran.wordpress.com/2013/05/04/the-author-exploitation-business/

Writer Beware on Facebook
https://www.facebook.com/WriterBeware

Romance Covers
http://www.romancenovelcovers.com/

Covers of Ramona (my cover designer)
http://coversbyramona.blogspot.com/

A study by Smashwords
http://blog.smashwords.com/2013/05/new-smashwords-survey-helps-authors.html

Bitly to shorten links
http://bitly.com/

Email List
www.Mailchimp.com

Kindle ebook about formatting Kindle ebooks, by Kindle and free:

http://amzn.com/B007URVZJ6.

Author Central
www.authorcentral.amazon.com

ACX for audio books
https://www.acx.com/

The Writer's Resource Directory of reviewers
http://writersresourcedirectory.com/Book_Reviewers.html

The Best Book Reviewers on Twitter
http://www.mediabistro.com/galleycat/best-book-reviewers-on-twitter_b11136

"Self-Publishing Success Stories: The Anatomy of a Kindle Bestseller," by Mark Edwards.

http://www.thecreativepenn.com/2013/01/21/self-publishing-success-kindle-bestseller/

*If you find a link that no longer works or if you would like to send feedback or your success story, please email Kristen@writerkristenjames.com.

About The Author

Kristen James is a bestselling author of romance with a twist. Her other nonfiction books include *How to be a Full Time Writer* for freelancers and ghostwriters, and *Blockbuster Books, Broken Down*, which has a novel map and outlining worksheets.

www.writerkristenjames.com

www.facebook.com/WriterKristenJames

19143233R00074

Made in the USA
Middletown, DE
06 April 2015